AMAZING
METS TRIVIA

Ross Adell
and
Ken Samelson

TAYLOR TRADE PUBLISHING

Lanham • New York • Toronto • Oxford

This Taylor Trade Publishing paperback edition of *Amazing Mets Trivia* is an original publication. It is published by arrangement with the author.

Copyright © 2004 by Ross Adell and Ken Samelson
First Taylor Trade Publishing edition 2004

Published by Taylor Trade Publishing
An imprint of The Rowman & Littlefield Publishing Group, Inc.
4501 Forbes Boulevard, Suite 200
Lanham, Maryland 20706

Distributed by National Book Network

ISBN 1-58979-035-9

∞™ The paper used in this publication meets the minimum requirements of American National Standard for Information Sciences—Permanence of Paper for Printed Library Materials, ANSI/NISO Z39.48–1992.
Manufactured in the United States of America.

This book is dedicated to my mom, Phyllis Adell, whose favorite player was Gil Hodges; my dad, Al Adell, who took me to my first Met game in 1964; and my brother Fred Adell, who likes Yogi Berra and Casey Stengel. A very special dedication goes to my godson, Teddy Matthew Rose; his sister, Alicia Michelle Rose; and their parents, my very good friends, David and Beatrice Rose.

I also would like to dedicate this book to some people who have passed away, but their memories live forever. From the New York Mets family: Tommie Agee, Gil Hodges, Johnny Murphy, Lindsey Nelson, Joan Payson, and Casey Stengel. From SABR: Bob Davids, who founded the organization in 1971; Bob Garfinkle; Eddie Gold; Leonard Koppett; Bill Pechette; and William Ruiz.

Finally, I would like to mention two other people. Joe McLaughlin was an ardent Met fan who used to see the Mets play in Philadelphia and travel to Florida and see them in spring training. Joe passed away on March 17, 2003, and he will be missed. Thomas Casoria of Whitestone, Queens, was a firefighter with Engine Co. 22 in Manhattan and lost his life in the World Trade Center attack when he and two of his colleagues were carrying a paraplegic out of Tower One before the tower collapsed on September 11, 2001. Thomas was a graduate of Holy Cross High School in Flushing, New York, and was captain of his baseball team, where he played second base. He also was an all-city football player. He also was a very big Met fan. Rest in peace, Thomas!

CONTENTS

METS TRIVIA: The Managers

POSTSEASON YEARS

MISCELLANEOUS METS TRIVIA

ACKNOWLEDGMENTS

Baseball brings people together, no matter what you do for a living, no matter what age you are, and no matter what your background is. I would like to thank the following people who made contributions to this project, whether it was words of encouragement, material for the book, or just talking Met baseball with me.

My friends from the Society for American Baseball Research (SABR): Nic Antoine, Damian Begley, Rev. Gerald Beirne, John Bennett, Alex Bensky, John Blackburn, Burt Bloom, Al Blumkin, Arnie Braunstein, Patty Braunstein, Josh Burstein, Mike Caragliano, Clem Comly, Rory Costello, "Kit" Crissey, Bill Deane, Joe Dittmar, Morris Eckhouse, Rob Edelman, Eric Enders, Joe Favano, Sean Forman, Tom Forsaith, Mike Getz, Lynne Glickman, Phil Goldberg, "Duke" Goldman, "Woody" Goldstein, Mike Hayes, Elliot Hines, Tom Howell, Richard Hunt, Fred Ivor-Campbell, Doug Jacobs, Jane Jacobs, Lloyd Johnson, Cliff Kachline, Jerry Kahn, Mark Kanter, Seamus Kearney, Rich Klein, Alan Kleinberger, Tom Knight, Steve Krevisky, Len Levin, Howie Luloff, Ed Luteran, Matt McBride, Bob McConnell, Joe McGillen, Anthony Monti, Irv Mouallem, Steve Nadel, Tom Nahigian, Pete Palmer, Doug Pappas, John Pardon, Danny Price, Rob Rafal, Dave Raglin, George Robinson, David Rothenberg, Tom Ruane, Vince Russo, Scott Schleifer, Jeff Shames, Ira Siegel, Joe Simenic, Tom Simon, David W. Smith, Lyle Spatz, Greg Spira, Dick Thompson, Stew Thornley, Anne Tomczyk, Liz "Cookie" Tomczyk, Frank Vaccaro, Charlie Vascellaro, Dave Vincent, John Vorperian, Ty Waterman, Mike Webber, Bill Weber, Tim Wiles, John Zajc, Dave Zeman, and Tom Zocco.

A special thank-you to my coauthor, Ken Samelson, for letting me work on this project and to Scott Flatow, who came through in "the late innings" with some helpful suggestions.

My baseball friends and colleagues (past and present) from Citigroup, including Virginia Abrahamsen, Larry Acquaviva, Linda Aquino, Art Aronovitz, Kent Atkinson, Joan Austin, Mike Austin, Silvia Baptiste, Surretta Barnes, M. J. Batchelor, Steve Battaglia, Waldemar Bento, Chuck Berl, Gina Blander, Kenia Borges, Mari Brill, Carl Brome, Amy Brout, Darren Buck, Carlyle Callender, Guillermo Campelo, Cecil

Clacken, Charles Cona, Margaret Culkin, Joe Dabovich, Patricia Dizon, Regina Drollinger, Evelyn Dueno, Jorge Ferreira, Janet Frachtenberg, Sal Frosina, Angelo Fusaro, Josefina Garcia, William Garnes, Brent Geller, Evelyn Gonzalez, Adele Gorman, Edwin Guzman, Susan Hanyen, Rosaline Hazelwood, Leon Hendricks, Claribel Herrera, Rob Jackson, Harry Jobes, Isabel Khan, Hilda Kulkarni, Francois Larche, Kevin Lau, Donna Lent, Joel Levenberg, Ron Loiola, Mr. Richard Ludwig, Steve Lynch, Diane MacCarrick, Jim Mack, Bob Mallek, Helen Mardesic, John Martinez, Lou Mastandrea, Cecilia Mata, Bernadette McKevitt, Marilyn McNulty, Sonia Mendez, Al Minervini, Norma Moreno, Kathy Morgan, Radhika Navaratnarajah, Sophie Nikolos, Mary O'Brien, Deb O'Neil, Marjorie Oquendo-Pai, Helen Pak, Ed Pantina, Marianne Perez-Fernandez, Robert Petrowsky, Josephine Piazza, Maria Piccino, Kalman Pipo, Joanne Polichetti, Leon Rabouine, Caridad Ramos, Louis Rivera, Elizabeth Rodriguez, Mary Rodriguez, Angela Romero, Marisol Rosero-Jurado, Mike Ruiz, Susana Ruiz, Edgardo Santiago, Julio Santos, Rolf Schmelzer, Linda Schuster, Luciano Senger, Jorge Severiano, Hyundae Shin, Mark Silverman, Annie Lisa Smith, Sharron Smith, Rosemarie Smith-Williams, Gene Smothers, Maria Solorzano, Paulo de Souza, Barrett Stokes, Steve de la Vega, Nitza Vicente, Angel Villanueva, Ronnie Wackstein, Laura Weiner, and Rupert West.

I would like to acknowledge some of my friends with whom I used to talk baseball or hang out during my youth at Shea Stadium: Robert Abrams, Matt Amitrano, Joe Baumgarten, Glen Datz, David Donaldson, Tevyen Dorfman, Bob Hoepfner, Alan Isaacson, Lloyd Katz, Danny Lebenstein, Larry Mischell, Richard Romm, Ed Schwartz, Sheldon Stoller, and David Wolfson.

I would also like to acknowledge some of my baseball fan friends with whom I became friendly as an adult: Robert Begley, Vinny Casoria, Phil Cavaliere, Richie Chazen, Jane Christman, John Connelly, Vincent Dunn, Mark Ensling, Gary Gregory, Barry Rogers, Frank Siciliano, Paul Tycott, Howie Wasserman, and Matt and Trudee Wynn. A special thank-you to Dave and Linda Kreischer, and the entire Kreischer family, for making me feel at home when I stayed at their house in Chicago, which is a ten-minute walk from Wrigley Field. Also I want to thank the Rose-Donnelly-Belcore family for always making me feel welcome.

Also my thanks to some of the people who helped put this book together, including Matthew Fulks, Jill Langford, Jed Lyons, Erin McKindley, Tracy Miracle, Nancy Rothschild, and Bob Snodgrass.

METS TRIVIA:
The Players

TOMMIE AGEE

1 This man, who was born exactly five days before Agee, was a teammate of Agee both at Mobile County Training High School in Alabama and as a member of the Mets. Who is he?

2 What African American college that currently plays basketball in the Southwestern Athletic Conference did Agee attend before he signed with the Cleveland Indian organization?

3 What year did Agee win the American League Rookie of the Year award as a member of the Chicago White Sox?

4 The Mets acquired Agee from the White Sox on December 15, 1967, for outfielder Tommy Davis, pitchers Jack Fisher and Billy Wynne, and minor league catcher Buddy Booker. What other player did the Mets receive from the "Pale Hose" in this deal?

5 In Agee's first at bat in spring training (March 9, 1968), he was beaned by which St. Louis Cardinal Hall of Fame pitcher?

6 Agee went hitless in thirty-four consecutive at bats, tying Don Zimmer's 1962 record. Agee's streak ended on May 1, 1968, when he singled against a Phillie pitcher who had a 21–2 lifetime record against the Mets. Can you name this Met nemesis?

7 Agee did become a hero on May 16, 1968, when he drove in the winning run with a single in the bottom of the ninth inning for a 2–1 victory over the Cincinnati Reds, giving Tom Seaver the victory. What outfielder who had a lifetime .157 batting average for the Mets in ninety-four games in 1967 and 1968 scored the winning run, and who was the losing pitcher for the Reds, who pitched for the Mets in 1966?

8 Agee is the only player in Shea Stadium history (through the 2002 season) to hit a home run in the left field upper deck. The Montreal Expo pitcher who allowed Agee's "monster" shot on April 10, 1969, shut out the Los Angeles Dodgers in five starts in 1966 as a member of the St. Louis Cardinals. Name him.

9 On June 4, 1969, Agee scored the only run of the game in the bottom of the fifteenth inning against the Dodgers. Agee was on first base and scored when Wayne Garrett's single was misplayed by this Dodger center fielder. Name him.

10 Agee bounced back from his disappointing 1968 season as he led the 1969 World Champion Mets in home runs with how many?

11 On July 6, 1970, Agee became the second player in Met history to hit for the cycle. Against what team did Agee accomplish this feat?

12 On July 24, 1970, the Mets beat the Dodgers, 2–1 at Shea Stadium as Agee stole home in the bottom of the tenth for the winning run. Who was the Dodger relief pitcher who specialized in throwing the screwball, against whom Agee stole home?

13 Agee was the first Met to score over a hundred runs in a season in 1970. How many runs did he score in 1970?

14 On September 23, 1973, while playing for the St. Louis Cardinals, Agee slugged the last home run of his career. Ironically, it was against the Mets at Shea Stadium. Name the left-handed Met pitcher who allowed the 130th and final home run of Agee's career.

15 Agee's first major league skipper managed the Cleveland Indians in 1962 and the Kansas City Athletics in 1964 and part of 1965. He also played for the New York Knickerbockers of the National Basketball Association in the 1948–1949 season. Who is he?

EDGARDO ALFONZO

1 Alfonzo collected his first major league hit, a double on May 2, 1995, in a 9–6 loss to the Expos at Olympic Stadium. Name the Montreal pitcher with a 13–14 record as a starter in 1995 who gave up Alfonzo's initial hit.

2 "Fonzie" played in fifty-eight games at third base in 1995, and on May 2, he became the hundredth third baseman in Met history. Five other players appeared at third base in 1995, but only one of them played in more than forty games. Can you name him?

3 On May 6, 1995, Alfonzo slugged his first major league home run (inside the park) in Cincinnati. The relief pitcher who allowed the home run was pitching in only his second major league game. Name him.

4 Besides Alfonzo, three other Met players had inside-the-park homers for their first major league "dinger." Can you name this trio?

5 During the 1997 season, Alfonzo had his longest career hitting streak. How many games did Fonzie's hitting streak last?

6 Edgardo hit his first regular season grand slam on August 14, 1997, against which St. Louis Cardinal southpaw who went 3–7 in fourteen games in 1997?

7 Alfonzo hit his first career leadoff home run on April 16, 1998, against the Cubs at Shea Stadium. The Cub pitcher who allowed the homer pitched for the Mets in 1989. Can you name him?

8 Edgardo homered in a 1–0 game versus St. Louis in the second game of a doubleheader at Shea on August 21, 1998. Which Cardinal pitcher surrendered the homer?

9 With twenty-seven home runs and 108 RBIs in 1999, Alfonzo set records for Met second basemen. Which former Met "keystone sacker" held the previous record with twenty-one homers and eighty RBIs in 1993?

10 Alfonzo set a team record by scoring 123 runs in 1999. Who held the previous record with 117?

11 What are the most hits that Alfonzo collected in a season?

12 Edgardo had the most productive game of his career against Houston at The Astrodome on August 30, 1999. He went 6–6 with a double, three home runs (which tied a Met record), and had five RBIs. He thus became the first Met to garner six hits in a game. What other two individual game Met records did he set that night?

13 How many seasons has Alfonzo hit over .300?

14 Fonzie drove in the winning run in the last of the ninth inning with a single to give the Mets an 8–7 win in the first game of a doubleheader on August 22, 1999, against the Cardinals at Shea. The Mets were trailing 6–1 when they came to bat in the bottom of the eighth. Which St. Louis pitcher did Alfonzo get the winning hit against?

15 In 2002, Fonzie hit .308 while playing third base and finished tenth in the National League batting race. What Met third baseman hit .304 in 1977 while playing 110 games at third base?

16 Edgardo wore uniform number 13 in honor of a fellow Venezuelan who played with the same National League team from 1970 to 1988. Who is this nineteen-year veteran infielder?

17 On August 28, 1996, in a game against San Diego, Edgardo was the 2,000th career strikeout victim of a former Los Angeles pitcher who spent eleven years as a Dodger from 1980 to 1990, compiling 141 victories. Who is this native of Mexico?

WALLY BACKMAN

1 In what year was Backman a first-round draft pick of the Mets in the June free agent draft?

2 Backman collected his first major league hit on September 2, 1980, at Dodger Stadium in his first major league at bat. The pitcher who allowed Backman's initial hit won twenty games in 1977 for the Minnesota Twins. Can you name him?

3 The Atlanta Brave hurler who served up Backman's first career home run on May 26, 1982, hit his only major league homer on July 4, 1985, against the Mets. Can you name him?

4 Backman only hit ten career home runs, but one was an inside-the-park home run at Shea on July 31, 1982, against Pittsburgh. The Pirate pitcher who allowed Backman's homer hit a grand slam against the Mets two years earlier. Can you name him?

5 On August 3, 1982, in a game at Wrigley Field, Wally was part of the fifth triple play turned by the Mets in their history. Who were the other two Met infielders involved in the triple play on the ball hit by Larry Bowa?

6 Backman drove in the winning run in the bottom of the twelfth inning in a game at Shea on July 23, 1984, against the Cardinals' Neil Allen. Which Met catcher scored the winning run for the Mets in their 4–3 win over St. Louis?

7 On July 20, 1984, Backman tied a Met record by slugging three doubles in one game. His third double was in the top of the eleventh inning in a 2–2 tie against the Reds at Riverfront Stadium. Wally was bunted over to third base and scored the winning run on a sacrifice fly by which Met?

8 In 1984, Backman had his most productive year in stealing bases. How many did he steal?

9 What year did Backman lead the Mets in stolen bases with thirty?

10 In a 6–0 victory over the Pirates at Shea on April 26,1985, Wally tied a Met record with five hits in a game. Prior to Backman, the last time a Met garnered five hits in a game was in 1983. Can you name the two-term Met who accomplished this feat?

11 Backman drove in the only run in a 1–0 game at Montreal on August 19, 1985, with a double in the eighth inning. Name the losing pitcher for the Expos who hurled for the Mets in 1991 and 1992.

12 What year did Backman lead all National League second basemen in fielding percentage (.989)?

13 Backman hit into the sixth triple play in Met history on April 21, 1987, against the Pirates. Who were the two Met base runners who were erased?

14 Backman hit his tenth and last career home run on June 9, 1990, as a member of the Pittsburgh Pirates (ironically at Shea). The Met pitcher who allowed the home run was a teammate of Wally in 1987 and 1988 and had two tours of duty as a Met. Can you name him?

15 What American League team did Wally finish his career with in 1993?

GARY CARTER

1 What is Carter's nickname?

2 What Hall of Fame pitcher served up Carter's first major league home run on September 28, 1974?

3 On May 10, 1981, Carter was the Montreal catcher when this Expo pitcher no-hit the Giants, 4–0, for the first no-hitter pitched at Olympic Stadium. Can you name this pitcher who was born in Orleans, France?

4 In the 1981 All-Star Game in Cleveland, Carter garnered Most Valuable Player honors by smacking two home runs in a 5–4 National League victory. Name the two American League pitchers whom Carter homered against.

5 Carter came to the Mets on December 10, 1984, in a trade with the Montreal Expos. The Expos received four players from the Mets. Can you name this quartet?

6 Carter had a spectacular Met debut on April 9, 1985, in a game against the St. Louis Cardinals at Shea. Carter homered with one out in the bottom of the tenth inning to give the Mets a 6–5 victory. The Cardinal pitcher who delivered the home run had pitched for the Mets from 1979 to 1983. Who is he?

7 Three days later on April 12, 1985, Gary drove in the only run in a 1–0 Met win over Cincinnati with a home run in the fourth inning. The Red pitcher who surrendered Carter's blast led the National League in complete games in 1983 and 1984. Who is this "workhorse"?

8 On July 4, 1985, Carter tied a Met record with five hits in a wild and wacky nineteen-inning game, which the Mets won 16–13. With the score tied at 11–11, Carter scored the go-ahead run in the top of the nineteenth on a double by which future Met World Series hero?

9 On September 3 and 4, 1985, Carter became the first Met and the thirteenth player in major league history to smack five homers in two consecutive games. Against which team did Carter accomplish this feat?

10 On August 16, 1986, Carter injured his thumb while fielding a ground ball at first base and had to go on the disabled list. Which Cardinal backstop who also caught for the Phillies, Pirates, and White Sox hit the grounder that shelved Carter for fifteen days?

11 In 1986, Carter led the Mets with 105 runs batted in and in doing so tied a Met record that was originally set in 1975 by what Met outfielder?

12 In the fifth game of the 1986 National League Championship Series, Gary drove in the winning run in the bottom of the twelfth inning with a single, giving the Mets a 2–1 victory and a three games to two lead. Which Met infielder scored the winning run?

13 Gary hit his hundredth career home run against the Mets on May 10, 1980, against a pitcher who won twenty-two games for Vancouver of the Pacific Coast League in 1979. Who is this pitcher who was acquired from the Milwaukee Brewers?

14 In addition, Carter smacked his two hundredth career home run against the Mets on June 9, 1984. The pitcher who gave up this homer pitched for the Yankees in the 1977 World Series. Name him.

15 Carter smacked his three hundredth career home run on August 11, 1988, at Wrigley Field and became the fifty-ninth major leaguer to reach the three hundred home run plateau. The Cub pitcher that allowed Carter's milestone shot also gave up a home run to Carter in the 1986 World Series. Can you name him?

16 While playing for the San Francisco Giants on May 2, 1990, Gary slugged his only career pinch home run in the ninth inning in a 9–6 loss to the Chicago Cubs. This relief pitcher who surrendered Carter's pinch blast pitched for five teams including the Yankees in a fourteen-year major league career. Can you name him?

17 Gary is the National League all-time leader in games caught with 2,056 games behind the plate. What Hall of Famer who played with the Dodgers, Braves, and Pirates had the previous National League record with 1,861 games caught?

18 Gary is one of four players in major league history whose primary position was catcher to attain at least two thousand hits, one thousand runs batted in, one thousand runs scored, and three hundred home runs. Who are the other three?

19 Carter was elected to the Baseball Hall of Fame in January 2003. One of his teammates from the 1991 Los Angeles Dodgers was also elected that same day. Can you name this slugging first baseman who played twenty-one seasons, including the Mets in 1992 and 1993?

20 Carter's highest batting average for one season was in 1984. What did Gary hit that year?

21 Gary made his major league debut against the Mets in the second game of a twi-night doubleheader on September 16, 1974. He was the starting catcher, hit seventh, and went hitless in four at bats. Ironically, the Met starting pitcher in that game also made his major league debut and recorded his only big league victory. Who is this first pick of the June 1969 draft?

22 Two days later, on September 18, 1974, Carter appeared as a pinch hitter for Expo pitcher Steve Rogers in the seventh inning and delivered his first big league hit. The Met pitcher who allowed Carter's initial hit hurled for the Mets from 1971 to 1977. Who is he?

23 Gary Carter and Steve Rogers combined to be the starting battery at the 1982 All-Star Game (ASG), which was held at Olympic Stadium in Montreal. They became the first starting battery of a host city of an ASG since the second ASG of 1960 when it was held at an American League city. Name the starting AL battery for that game and the ballpark.

24 Carter registered his thousandth career hit on August 17, 1982, against the Atlanta Braves. Can you name the Brave hurler who also pitched with the Phillies and the Pirates who allowed the hit?

25 Which catcher did the Expos trade to the Phillies in 1977 to enable Carter to become the Expos' regular backstop?

26 Gary hit a total of 324 career home runs. As a catcher, he belted 298 round-trippers, which is sixth best in major league history going into the 2003 season. The catcher who is in fifth place on the list hit 299 homers as a backstop and also hit 324 lifetime homers. Name this nineteen-year veteran receiver who made his debut in 1977 and spent the majority of his career in the American League.

DAVID CONE

1 Cone registered his first major league victory on May 12, 1987, a 6–2 complete game win over the Cincinnati Reds at Riverfront Stadium. The losing pitcher in that game for the Reds toiled in the majors from 1969 to 1990. Can you name this four-decade pitcher?

2 On May 27, 1987, Cone fractured a finger on his right hand trying to bunt in a game at Candlestick Park in San Francisco. Who was the Giant pitcher whom Cone was attempting to bunt against?

3 In 1988, Cone had a 20–3 record and won his final eight starting assignments in a row, tying a Met record. Two other pitchers in Met history have won eight games in eight consecutive starts. Can you name this pair?

4 Cone's three losses in 1988 were the fewest by a National League twenty-game winner since a Brooklyn pitcher went 22–3 in 1951. Who is this Dodger southpaw?

5 Cone's earned run average (ERA) in 1988 was a sparkling 2.22, but he finished second in the National League. Which Cardinal hurler led the National League in ERA in 1988?

6 On August 1, 1990, Cone became the first Met pitcher to record a pinch hit as he singled in the top of the eleventh inning off the Expos' Dale Mohorcic in a game that the Mets would eventually win, 6–4 in twelve innings. Which pitcher did Cone bat for?

7 Cone, on August 30, 1991, struck out the side on nine pitches in the fifth inning against the Cincinnati Reds. One of the three batters fanned was Mariano Duncan. The other two played for the Mets at one time in their careers. Can you name this pair?

8 On April 28, 1992, the Mets won 4–0 at Shea as Cone had a no-hitter broken up with one out in the eighth inning against the Houston Astros. The batter who spoiled Cone's no-hitter pinch-hit for relief pitcher Rob Murphy. Can you name this Brooklyn-born first baseman/outfielder who also played for the Pirates for four years in the 1980s?

9 Prior to the 2003 season, Cone is one of four hurlers to start games for the Mets, Yankees, and Boston Red Sox. Who are the other three?

10 Which two consecutive seasons did Cone lead the National League in strikeouts?

11 On June 18, 1997, at Yankee Stadium, in only the third regular season game ever between the Mets and the Yankees, David fanned eleven Mets and had a no-hitter for six innings until which Met doubled to lead off the seventh inning?

12 Five days later on June 23, 1997, Cone fanned sixteen Tigers to set a new Yankee record for most strikeouts in one game by a Yankee right-handed pitcher. Who had the old mark of fifteen, which was set on September 27, 1919?

13 Cone's first tenure as a Met ended on August 27, 1992, when he was traded to Toronto for which two players?

14 Cone won the American League Cy Young Award in 1994 as a member of what team?

15 Cone pitched a perfect game for the Yankees on July 18, 1999, against the Montreal Expos at Yankee Stadium. Which Expo infielder made the final out?

16 Cone only faced one Met hitter in the 2000 World Series (game 4). Who was the batter Cone faced?

17 Through 2002, how many times has Cone played with a World Series winning team during his career?

18 On September 2, 1996, after a four-month layoff due to a small aneurysm in the upper part of his right arm, Cone returned to the

Yankees and pitched seven hitless innings as he combined with Mariano Rivera for a one-hit, 5–0 victory. Against which team did Cone pitch in his comeback?

19 What two uniform numbers did Cone wear during his first tour of duty with the Mets?

20 David returned to the Mets on April 4, 2003, and pitched five scoreless innings and was the winning pitcher in a 4–0 win over the Montreal Expos. He allowed two hits, both to the opposing starting pitcher. Who is this native of Japan?

RON DARLING

1 What Ivy League school did Darling attend?

2 In 1981, Darling lost to St. John's University in an NCAA Regional play-off game, 1–0 in twelve innings, despite pitching a no-hitter for eleven innings. The winning pitcher for St. John's became a Met teammate of Darling from 1989 to 1991. Who is he?

3 The Mets acquired Darling from the Texas Rangers on April 1, 1982, along with pitcher Walt Terrell. Who did the Mets trade to the Rangers to obtain Darling and Terrell?

4 Darling won his first major league game on September 28, 1983, at Three Rivers Stadium. The losing pitcher for the Pirates won eleven games in 1983 for the "Buccos." Can you name him?

5 Darling's career high as a Met for most strikeouts in a game is twelve. He accomplished this twice, on August 29, 1984, and May 27, 1986. Ironically, it was against the same team both times. Name this team.

6 In what year was Darling selected for the National League All-Star Team?

7 Darling appeared in relief for the first time in his major league career in the wild game of July 4, 1985, as he pitched the nineteenth inning in a 16–13 Met victory in Atlanta. The pitcher whom Darling replaced hurled six innings and got credit for the victory, as the Mets scored five times in the top of the nineteenth. Name this winning pitcher.

8 On October 1, 1985, Darling pitched a masterful game in St. Louis as the Mets won 1–0 in eleven innings on Darryl Strawberry's home run. Darling pitched nine innings of shutout ball, allowing four hits and three walks while striking out five and got a no-decision. The win left the Mets two games back of the Cardinals with five games to play. Who was the Cardinal starter who threw ten innings of shutout ball?

9 Darling posted his lowest earned run average as a Met and finished third in the National League in ERA in 1986. What was Darling's ERA in that championship season?

10 On June 28, 1987, against the Phillies at Veterans Stadium, Darling had a no-hitter through seven innings. The leadoff batter for the Phillies in the eighth ruined Darling's bid to become the first Met to hurl a no-hitter with a pinch-hit triple. Can you name this pinch-hitting specialist who had 143 career pinch hits?

11 Darling tore ligaments in his right thumb on September 11, 1987, while diving for a bunt against the Cardinals, which ended his season. The St. Louis batter who hit the grounder was a Met teammate of Darling in 1991. Who is he?

12 What were the most victories that Darling garnered in one season as a Met?

13 Darling hit the only two home runs of his career in consecutive starts in 1989. He hit one on June 24 against the Phillies and one on June 30 against the Reds. Who were the two pitchers Ron homered against?

14 Darling is the only Met pitcher to win a Golden Glove Award for fielding excellence. What year did he win this award?

15 Darling is fourth on the all-time Met list in career wins. How many victories does he have?

16 Darling was chosen by the Texas Rangers as the ninth pick in the first round in the June 1981 amateur draft. The fourth pick (Mets), the sixth pick (Padres), and the seventh pick (White Sox) all selected players who would eventually be New York Met teammates of Ron. Can you name this trio of outfielders?

LENNY DYKSTRA

1 What is Dykstra's nickname?

2 Dykstra homered in the first game of his major league career, in his second at bat at Riverfront Stadium in Cincinnati on May 3, 1985. Which Red pitcher gave up Dykstra's first "circuit clout"?

3 Lenny is the co-leader of the Met record for career home runs leading off a game. How many did he hit, and whom is he tied with?

4 What year did Dykstra lead the Mets in both triples and stolen bases?

5 What was Dykstra's highest batting average as a Met?

6 Dykstra hit two home runs in a game for the Mets on May 23, 1987, against the Dodgers. He connected twice against a Los Angeles pitcher who would later win the Cy Young Award in the American League in 1990. Can you name him?

7 Lenny hit his only career grand slam on September 16, 1987, in the eighth inning at Montreal in a 10–0 Met victory. Can you name the pitcher who went 6–15 that season for the Expos as both a starter and reliever who allowed Lenny's grand slam?

8 In 1987, Dykstra hit thirty-seven doubles to tie a Met record. Who were the two Mets that had thirty-seven doubles in a season when Dykstra tied the record?

9 On April 14, 1988, Dykstra homered in the fourth inning against the Expos at Shea for the only run in a 1–0 game. Lenny homered against a pitcher who would pitch a perfect game three years later. Can you name this hurler who allowed a total of four homers to Dykstra, the most Lenny had against any pitcher?

10 Lenny hit the first "official" home run at a night game at Wrigley Field on August 9, 1988, against a Cub pitcher who led the National League in winning percentage in 1989. Can you name this pitcher who toiled for five teams, including three times with the Atlanta Braves?

11 Lenny had one inside-the-park home run in his career, and it came against the Mets on July 24, 1990, at Veterans Stadium. Who was the Met pitcher?

12 Dykstra led the major leagues in runs scored in 1993 with 143. It was the most runs scored by a National Leaguer since what Hall of Famer (also with the Phillies) had 152 runs scored in 1932?

13 In 1993, Dykstra led the National League in both hits and walks, and he reached base 325 times. He became the first National Leaguer to reach base 300 times since what outfielder reached base 303 times in 1987?

14 Lenny had the most home runs of any player who participated in the 1993 World Series, won by Toronto, four games to two. How many home runs did he hit?

15 Lenny homered in his final World Series at bat in the sixth and deciding game of the 1993 series. He homered off a pitcher who had four consecutive seasons of twenty or more victories from 1987 to 1990 with Oakland. Can you name this right-hander?

16 On April 16, 1996, Dykstra hit his eighty-first and last career home run against the Montreal Expos' Jose Paniagua. It was a leadoff shot. The following batter also homered to give the Phillies a quick 2–0 lead. Who is this two-term Phillie infielder who followed Dykstra?

SID FERNANDEZ

1 Fernandez came to the Mets from the Dodgers with infielder Ross Jones on December 8, 1983. Which two players did the Mets trade to Los Angeles in that deal?

2 Sid was born in Honolulu, Hawaii, and wore uniform number 50. What other Met player was born in Honolulu and wore number 50?

3 Sid won his first game in the majors on July 16, 1984, five days after being recalled from Tidewater of the International League. He defeated the Astros, 13–3. The losing pitcher for Houston was a former Met. Name him.

4 On May 11, 1985, Sid combined with Roger McDowell to one-hit the Phillies, 4–0. Who got the only hit for the Phillies?

5 What was the only season that Fernandez reached the two hundred strikeout mark?

6 What year did Fernandez lead the Mets' pitchers with eleven hits?

7 What were the most victories Sid compiled in one season?

8 Fernandez is the only player in Met history to collect three sacrifice hits in one game. He did this on July 24, 1987, in the first game of a doubleheader against what team?

9 Fernandez registered his only career save on October 5, 1986. Who was the Met winning pitcher in that game?

10 On June 25, 1989, Fernandez pitched seven innings and defeated the Phillies at Shea, 5–1. In this game, the Mets tied a major league record and set a National League record when they did not record any assists in that game. The losing pitcher for Philadelphia played for the Phillies on two separate occasions as well as the Cubs twice and the Giants three times. Who is this pitcher who hurled a no-hitter against the Giants on August 15, 1990, as a member of the Phillies?

11 What two seasons did Sid lead the Mets in earned run average?

12 Fernandez had the lowest opponent's batting average against in the National League for which three seasons?

13 Fernandez stroked his only career home run on September 21, 1989, against the St. Louis Cardinals. The pitcher that gave up Sid's "dinger" led the American League in saves for four consecutive years from 1982 to 1985. Who was this closer who died in 1998?

14 How many complete-game shutouts did Sid have in his major league career?

15 On July 14, 1989, Sid set a Met record for most strikeouts in a game by a Met left-handed pitcher when he fanned sixteen Braves. Unfortunately the Mets lost the game, 3–2, in the bottom of the ninth inning on a home run by the Brave left fielder. Can you name this man who also played for the Phillies, Cardinals, Royals, Pirates, and Orioles from 1978 to 1994?

16 In the seventh and deciding game of the 1986 World Series, Sid relieved Ron Darling in the fourth inning. Sid walked the first batter he faced (Wade Boggs) but then retired the next seven batters, four of them by strikeouts. Who were the four batters whom Fernandez fanned?

JOHN FRANCO

1 What National League team selected John in the June 1981 free agent draft?

2 The Brooklyn high school that Franco graduated from was the same high school that Hall of Famer Sandy Koufax attended. Can you name this school?

3 Franco attended college at St. John's University. Which early-day Met who led the team in saves in 1963 also attended St. John's?

4 In the first game of a doubleheader on April 29, 1984, Franco recorded his first career save as the Reds defeated the Giants, 8–1. The winning pitcher for Cincinnati pitched for the Mets from 1984 to 1986. Can you name this pitcher?

5 Franco's longest career winning streak took place in 1985 as a member of the Cincinnati Reds. How many consecutive games did he win?

6 What are the most games that Franco won in one season as a Met?

7 In 1994, Franco set a major league record for career saves for left-handed pitchers. This sixteen-year veteran who pitched eleven years for the Yankees before spending three seasons with San Francisco from 1991 to 1993 held the previous mark with 252 saves. Who is this southpaw?

8 Franco recorded his four hundredth save on April 14, 1999, against the Florida Marlins, becoming the second major league pitcher to accomplish this feat. What former Cy Young Award winner (with another team) was the winning pitcher for the Mets in that historic game?

9 Franco has appeared in the most games as a pitcher in Met history, with 605 appearances through the 2002 season, all in relief. Do you know which pitcher is second in team history with 269 appearances, without being a starting pitcher for the Mets?

10 Franco led the National League in saves in which three seasons?

11 Franco holds the all-time Met career record for saves with how many going into the 2003 season?

12 Going into the 2003 season, Franco leads all active relief pitchers with 422 saves. Can you name this right-hander who began his major league career in 1993 and is in second place with 352 saves?

13 Franco, with 422 career saves through the 2002 season, is second on the all-time save list. Who has the most career saves with 478?

14 With his 422 saves, John has the most career saves by a left-handed pitcher. The leftie reliever who is in second place with 347 saves among southpaws started his career as a Met in 1985 and ironically was involved in the trade with the Reds that brought Franco to the Mets. Name him.

15 As a Met, Franco had two seasons with an earned run average of less than 2.00. Can you name the years?

16 Who was John's first major league manager with Cincinnati?

17 In 1992, John was limited to thirty-one games due to an elbow injury and was put on the disabled list twice. However, he still managed to share the team lead in saves that year (fifteen) with which right-handed pitcher?

DWIGHT GOODEN

1 Dwight was a first-round pick in the June 1982 free agent draft. He was the fifth pick in the entire country. The Chicago Cubs had the first pick and selected a Brooklyn-born shortstop who played for the Mets for the last two months of the 1999 season. Can you name this graduate of Brooklyn's Thomas Jefferson High School?

2 Doc attended Hillsborough High School in Tampa, Florida. Can you name the Mets' first-round pick in 1971 who also attended Hillsborough High and who went hitless in ten at bats in four games for the Mets in 1974, his only major league season?

3 Ironically, the Mets' second pick in the June 1982 draft also attended Hillsborough High and is a close personal friend of Doc's. Can you name this hurler who started his major league career with Montreal in 1985?

4 Doc made his major league debut against the Houston Astros on April 7, 1984, in the Astrodome. This Houston shortstop led the National League in triples with ten in 1982 and became Doc's first major league strikeout victim. Who is he?

5 Doc had a no-hitter through seven innings against the Pirates on June 6, 1984. Which Pirate outfielder who was born in Canada led off the eighth inning with a single and broke up Gooden's no-hit bid?

6 Doc hit his first career home run on September 21, 1985, against the Pirates at Shea. The pitcher who allowed Gooden's homer also hurled for the Dodgers, Yankees, and Astros in his sixteen-year major league career. Name him.

7 Gooden set a club record by winning fourteen consecutive games in 1985. Tom Seaver had the old mark, which was set in 1969. How many games did Seaver win in a row?

8 Gooden's fourteen-game winning streak ended in San Francisco when he lost to the Giants, 3–2, on August 31, 1985. The Giant hurler who defeated Gooden on that day also pitched with Toronto and Los Angeles and had two separate stints with the Pirates in a career that ended in 1995. Who is he?

9 Gooden's ERA of 1.53 in 1985 was the lowest ERA in the majors since what Hall of Fame pitcher posted an ERA of 1.12 in 1968?

10 On August 25, 1985, Doc won his twentieth game of the season, becoming the youngest modern pitcher to win twenty. He was twenty years, nine months and nine days old. Prior to Gooden, who was the youngest in major league history to win twenty?

11 In 1985, Doc led the major leagues in wins (24), strikeouts (268), and ERA (1.53). He became the first pitcher to lead the majors in the "Triple Crown of Pitching" since what Hall of Famer did it in his final season in 1966?

12 Doc hurled a Met record eight shutouts in 1985 and finished second in the league. Which pitcher hurled ten shutouts and led the National League?

13 Gooden's first start after his drug rehab was on June 5, 1987, at Shea Stadium. A crowd of 51,402 were on hand to welcome Doc on his return. The Mets beat the Pirates that night, 5–1, as Gooden allowed four hits in 6⅔ innings. The first "Bucco" batter struck out to start the game. Can you name this Pirate?

14 In that game, the opposing starting pitcher for the Pirates made his major league debut. Can you name this Pirate freshman who won thirteen games in 1987 and finished second in the 1987 National League Rookie of the Year voting behind San Diego's Benito Santiago?

15 Doc became the third Met pitcher to reach the 1,500 strikeout plateau on July 11, 1991, against the San Diego Padres when he struck out this former teammate. Can you name this infielder who played for the Mets from 1986 to 1991?

16 Gooden pitched the first Opening Day complete-game shutout in Met history on April 5, 1993 (3–0), against the Colorado Rockies, who were playing their first game in their history. Can you name the Opening Day starting pitcher for the Rockies who was selected in the 1992 expansion draft from the Atlanta Braves roster?

17 On May 14, 1996, Gooden pitched a no-hitter against the Seattle Mariners in a 2–0 Yankee victory at Yankee Stadium. Which Mariner first baseman made the last out of the game?

18 From 1985 to 1994, Doc pitched in eight out of ten Opening Day games for the Mets, missing 1987 and 1992. Who were the two pitchers who started for the Mets on Opening Day those two seasons?

19 Before finishing his career in 2000 with his second tour of duty with the Yankees, what other two teams did Doc pitch with in 2000?

20 Can you name Dwight's nephew who started his major league career in 1988 with the Milwaukee Brewers and who has smacked 340 home runs through the 2002 season?

21 Gooden is in second place in the all-time Met strikeout list with how many?

22 Doc is also second in Met career wins. How many wins did Doc accumulate as a Met?

JERRY GROTE

1 On September 27, 1963, the Houston Colt 45's had an all-rookie starting lineup that included Jerry Grote. It was in this game that Grote collected his first major league hit. Ironically, it came against the Mets. Who was the Met pitcher who gave up Grote's first hit?

2 In that same all-rookie game, the Houston lineup included a future Met who played first base. Can you name him?

3 While with the Houston Colt 45's, on April 23, 1964, Grote caught a Houston pitcher who threw a no-hitter *but lost* to the Cincinnati Reds by a score of 1–0. Who is this losing no-hit pitcher who started his career with the Kansas City Athletics and who also pitched for the Reds, Braves, Cubs, Expos, and Yankees?

4 Grote smacked his first major league home run on June 26, 1964, against the Chicago Cubs. The pitcher who allowed Grote's initial circuit clout was a former World Series hero in the 1950s. Can you name him?

5 Grote is the only receiver in Met history to appear in over one thousand games. How many games did Grote catch as a Met?

6 Jerry's first major league manager played the outfield for the Cincinnati Reds from 1937 to 1942 and was the manager of Houston from 1962 to 1964. Who is he?

7 Grote's second inning single against Cincinnati on April 29, 1967, was the only hit this former Met pitcher allowed in a 7–0 shutout at Crosley Field. Who is this former Met pitcher?

8 Grote caught for the Mets from 1966 through part of the 1977 season when he was traded to the Dodgers. This 1961 expansion draftee was the Mets regular catcher in 1965 when he appeared in 112 games. Can you name him?

9 In a game at Jarry Park on May 18, 1970, Grote was the third of three Mets to hit consecutive home runs off Expo pitcher Bill Stoneman in the eighth inning. Who were the other two Mets to homer in this sequence?

10 In 1970, over a three-game span (July 7–July 9), Grote set a team record (since broken) for most consecutive hits in consecutive at bats with how many?

11 Grote ended a scoreless game by belting a home run in the bottom of the eleventh inning against the Cincinnati Reds on April 11, 1971, giving the Mets a 1–0 victory. The relief pitcher who gave up the home run pitched for seven different teams in his nine-year career, including a brief stint with the Yankees in 1973. Can you name him?

12 On July 20, 1971, Grote suffered a bruised chest when he collided with a brick wall at Wrigley Field while chasing a pop-up. The Cub batter who hit the ball played eight years as a New York Yankee, from 1962 to 1969. Can you name this controversial player?

13 Jerry smacked his first career grand slam on August 15, 1973, against this San Diego Padre pitcher who had a 34–67 career record, including losing twenty-one games for the Padres in 1972. Who is he?

14 Grote's only career pinch homer took place on July 4, 1975, in the top of the ninth inning at Veterans Stadium. The Mets were trailing the Phillies, 4–3; with a runner on second base, Grote homered off former teammate Tug McGraw to give the Mets a 5–4 win. Name the infielder that Grote pinch-hit for?

15 Grote caught twenty-two games for what American League West team in 1981?

16 On May 17, 1964, while with Houston, Jerry hit into a triple play against Philadelphia. Two of the three Phillie fielders who participated in the triple play were the first baseman, Johnny Hernstein, and the catcher, Gus Triandos. The other fielder was the shortstop and later was a coach for the Mets from 1993 to 1996. Can you name this twelve-year veteran who finished his career with the Expos in 1972?

17 During his major league career, Grote hit two home runs in a game only once. This took place on May 19, 1972, in Philadelphia. One of the pitchers Grote homered against was a former Met teammate from 1966 to 1968, while the other hurler won twenty games for the Phillies in 1966. Can you name this pair?

BUD HARRELSON

1 What is Bud Harrelson's given first name?

2 Harrelson was born on an important date in U.S. military history. What date?

3 Harrelson became the full-time Met shortstop in 1967. In 1966, two men shared the bulk of the Met shortstop duties. Name this pair.

4 In a game against the Atlanta Braves on July 9, 1967, Harrelson had four hits in four at bats but was pinch-hit for in the bottom of the ninth inning with the Mets trailing 4–3. The batter who substituted for Harrelson tied the game with a homer off Atlanta's Dick Kelley. (The Mets would win the game, 5–4.) Can you name this infielder who hit for Harrelson and was acquired by the Mets during spring training of 1967?

5 Harrelson's first major league home run was an inside-the-park homer at Forbes Field on August 17, 1967. Name the Pirate southpaw pitcher who allowed Harrelson's first home run and who pitched for the Milwaukee Braves against the Yankees in the 1957 and 1958 World Series.

6 On April 17, 1970, Harrelson hit his first over-the-fence home run against the Phillies. It would be the only Shea Stadium home run that he would ever hit. The Phillie southpaw who gave up this homer pitched briefly for the Yankees in 1976. Can you name the eighteen-year veteran who retired in 1982?

7 In 1970, Harrelson set a Met record (since broken) for most walks by a batter in a season. How many walks did Harrelson receive in 1970?

8 In a game at Dodger Stadium on April 26, 1970, Harrelson tied a team record when he became the second player in Met history to steal three bases in a game in a 3–1 Met victory. Can you name the early-day Met first baseman who was the first to accomplish this?

9 What year did Harrelson win his only Golden Glove Award?

10 On June 8, 1977, Harrelson became the third Met player to reach one thousand hits when he singled in the fifth inning against the Cincinnati Reds at Shea. The Red pitcher who gave up Harrelson's hit also allowed a historic home run in 1974. Can you name him?

11 What team did the Mets trade Harrelson to on March 23, 1978?

12 When Harrelson was traded, he was the Met career leader in what two offensive categories?

13 What team did Harrelson finish his playing career with?

14 How many games did the Mets win when Harrelson was their manager from 1990 to 1991?

15 When Harrelson was relieved of his managerial duties on September 29, 1991, who became the Mets interim manager?

16 On September 16, 1966, in a game at Candlestick Park, Harrelson stole home against San Francisco, giving the Mets a 5–3 lead. (The Mets eventually won the game, 5–4). The pitcher for the Giants when this occurred had a twenty-one-year major league career, including a stint with the Yankees from 1968 to 1973. Can you name this right-hander who also had a brother who pitched for the St. Louis Cardinals from 1957 to 1958?

17 Harrelson is one of three Mets who played in each World Series game in both 1969 and 1973. Can you name the other two?

KEITH HERNANDEZ

1 What is Keith's nickname?

2 Keith was selected in the June 1971 free agent draft by the St. Louis Cardinals in what round?

3 How many consecutive National League Golden Glove Awards did Keith win?

4 Hernandez belted his first career homer for the St. Louis Cardinals on May 24, 1975, against a Dodger pitcher who won at least thirteen games for Los Angeles from 1974 to 1978. Name this pitcher.

5 Keith smacked 162 lifetime home runs. His top victim allowed six home runs to him. Name this thirteen-year veteran pitcher who started his career with the Mets and pitched for New York from 1979 to 1982 before pitching for Houston.

6 Keith was co-MVP in the National League in 1979. Which Hall of Famer did he share the award with?

7 The only season that Keith had the highest batting average in the National League was in 1979. What was his average?

8 Keith set a Met record (since broken) by drawing ninety-seven walks in 1984. Who had the previous record of ninety-five, which was set in 1970?

9 Hernandez hit for the cycle on July 4, 1985, in a wild 16–13 win over the Braves that took nineteen innings to complete. Each hit was against a different pitcher. How many of the four pitchers can you name?

10 Prior to Keith, who was the last Met to hit for the cycle?

11 What was Keith's top home-run-hitting season?

12 In Keith's first three full seasons with the Mets (1984 to 1986), he hit over .300 in each of those three years. What were his batting averages during this period?

13 Keith collected his two thousandth career hit on September 15, 1987, against the Cubs at Shea. The Cub relief pitcher who allowed the hit started and ended his major league career with the Phillies, ten years apart (1982, 1992). Name him.

14 Keith's last major league season was 1990. Which team did he finish his career with?

15 Hernandez smacked his last career home run on April 25, 1990, against the Toronto Blue Jays. The pitcher who served up the home run had both a brother who pitched for the Royals and a father who pitched for the Yankees. Name him.

16 On May 8, 1977, Keith took part in a triple play against the Houston Astros. The other Cardinal fielders were second baseman Mike Tyson and shortstop Don Kessinger. The Houston batter was a Cardinal teammate of Keith's in 1976. Name this fourteen-year veteran who was with the Dodgers from 1964 to 1975.

TODD HUNDLEY

1 Hundley was the Mets' second pick in the June 1987 free agent draft. The Mets' first selection in that year's draft played in eighty-two games for the Mets in 1991 and 1992 before being chosen by the Florida Marlins in the expansion draft on November 17, 1992. Can you name this infielder?

2 In his major league debut, Todd recorded his first major league hit, a double on May 18, 1990, in the fourth inning against San Diego. The pitcher who allowed the hit started three games against the Mets in the 1986 World Series. Who is he?

3 Todd, the son of a major leaguer (Randy Hundley), smacked his first career homer on September 26, 1991, against a Pittsburgh Pirate pitcher whose father, Joe, also played in the majors in the 1950s, when he appeared in sixteen games with the Brooklyn Dodgers. Name the Pirate pitcher.

4 What other Met player besides Todd Hundley had a father who played for the Cubs?

5 Hundley was the Opening Day catcher for the Mets from 1992 to 1997. Who was the Opening Day catcher for the Mets in 1998?

6 Todd caught thirty-six games for the Mets in 1990. Which Met backstop caught the most games with eighty-seven in 1990?

7 Todd belted his first career grand slam on September 2, 1993, at Wrigley Field against a Cub pitcher who won at least ten games for the Texas Rangers in 1987, 1988, 1991, and 1992. Name him.

8 Todd hit a pinch grand slam on May 4, 1995, in Montreal against Expo relief pitcher Bryan Eversgerd in the tenth inning to give the Mets a 5–1 victory. Which Met relief pitcher did Todd bat for?

9 Hundley led the Mets in home runs in which two consecutive years?

10 Hundley broke a forty-three-year-old major league record in 1996 for most home runs by a catcher with forty-one. Which Brooklyn Dodger catcher had forty homers in 1953?

11 Todd hit his forty-first homer against an Atlanta Brave relief pitcher who would become a Met teammate of his in 1997 and 1998. Who was he?

12 In 1996, Hundley and this outfielder became the first pair of Mets to drive in at least one hundred runs in one season. Who was the outfielder?

13 In 1996, Todd became only the third switch-hitter in major league history to hit forty home runs in a season. Who were the first two?

14 In the first regular season game between the Mets and Yankees on June 16, 1997, which the Mets won, 6–0, Hundley stole home in the back end of a double steal in the first inning. Which Met was on the front end?

15 Todd was traded along with minor league pitcher Arnold Gooch in a three-team trade on December 1, 1998, that involved the Dodgers and the Orioles. Catcher Charles Johnson was also involved in that trade and wound up with the Orioles. What two players did the Mets receive in that deal?

16 On July 30, 1996, Todd hit a game-ending home run in the bottom of the twelfth inning as the Mets defeated the Pirates, 4–3. The Pirate pitcher who Todd homered against won twenty games for the Cubs in 2001. Who is he?

17 Todd holds the Met team record for most games with home runs from both sides of the plate. How many times did he accomplish this feat as a Met?

RON HUNT

1 From what organization did the Mets acquire Ron Hunt?

2 Who was the Met coach and former St. Louis Cardinal manager who recommended the Mets obtain Hunt?

3 In 1964, Hunt led the Mets in hitting. What was his batting average?

4 The Chicago Cub pitcher who allowed Hunt's first career home run on April 24, 1963, started his career with the Milwaukee Braves in 1953 and ended it with the Phillies in 1967. Who is this fifteen-year National League veteran who won a total of 166 games?

5 Hunt finished second in the 1963 National League Rookie of the Year Award. Who finished first?

6 How many home runs did Hunt smack in his rookie season?

7 Hunt belted the first Met home run at Shea Stadium on April 23, 1964, against a Chicago Cub pitcher who, after losing twenty games in 1962, won twenty-three games in 1963. Name this southpaw whose son pitched for the 1988 Red Sox.

8 In a 2–1 loss on May 4, 1964, at Milwaukee's County Stadium, Hunt was tagged out at home plate for the final out of the game. However, he got into an altercation and wrestling match with the Braves' catcher, which led to a full-scale brawl. Name the Braves catcher who also played for the Reds, Cubs, Angels, and twice with the San Francisco Giants.

9 What St. Louis Cardinal base runner collided with Hunt on May 11, 1965, which separated Hunt's left shoulder and kept Hunt from playing for nearly three months?

10 Which Hall of Fame pitcher gave up Hunt's only career inside-the-park home run on June 5, 1966?

11 On July 1, 1966, the Mets lost to the Pirates, 12–0, in a game at Shea. Hunt led off the bottom of the first inning with a single and then got caught stealing. The Pittsburgh hurler then retired the next twenty-six batters consecutively for a one-hit shutout. Can you name this Pirate southpaw who was a rookie in 1966?

12 Hunt holds the Met career record for getting hit by a pitched ball with how many?

13 While playing for the Montreal Expos, Hunt set a major league record for most times hit by a pitch in one season. How many times was he "plunked"?

14 On February 13, 1968, the Dodgers traded Hunt and infielder Nate Oliver to the Giants for a catcher who played twelve years in the big leagues from 1961 to 1972, finishing with the Detroit Tigers. Can you name this backstop whose brother umpired in the American League until 1982? (Note: This was the first trade between the Dodgers and the Giants since 1956 when the Brooklyn Dodgers traded Jackie Robinson to the New York Giants for pitcher Dick Littlefield, a trade that was subsequently canceled when Robinson announced his retirement.)

15 On September 28, 1965, Hunt drove in the winning run in the bottom of the twelfth inning with a base hit to beat Pittsburgh, 1–0. The Pirate relief pitcher who allowed the winning run pitched for the Buccos from 1953 to 1968 before being traded to the Tigers in 1968 and finishing with Montreal in 1969. Can you name this right-hander?

16 In the fourth inning of the second game of a doubleheader on May 19, 1963, against the Dodgers, Hunt was on third base with Chris Cannizzaro at the plate. On the first pitch, Hunt broke for home and scored as he knocked the ball out of the Los Angeles backstop's mitt. The result was an error to the catcher and *not* a stolen base. The pitcher subsequently faced the Mets in the 1969 World Series, and the catcher had a father who played in the National League with the Cubs, Phillies, and Dodgers from 1933 to 1943. Can you name this Dodger battery?

17 Hunt finished his major league career in 1974 with what National League team?

AL JACKSON

1 Jackson was born on Christmas Day 1935. From 1962 to 2002, there have been four Met players who also were born on December 25. Can you name the other four members of this "Christmas Quintet"?

2 In the National League expansion draft that was held on October 10, 1961, the Mets selected Jackson from which team?

3 Jackson led the Mets' staff in victories in 1963 with how many?

4 On July 21, 1965, against the Pirates at Forbes Field, Jackson had a no-hitter that was broken up with one out in the eighth inning. What Hall of Famer ended the no-hitter?

5 Jackson hit one home run in his major league career. Which Hall of Fame pitcher, who later became a Met in 1965, surrendered Jackson's only homer on July 26, 1964?

6 What was Jackson's nickname?

7 On October 20, 1965, Jackson's first tour of duty with the Mets ended as he and another player were traded to the St. Louis Cardinals for third baseman Ken Boyer. Who was the other player who went to St. Louis in exchange for Boyer?

8 Jackson held the Met record for most career victories by a pitcher until 1969 when Tom Seaver passed him. How many wins did Jackson register as a Met?

9 The Mets reacquired Jackson from St. Louis on October 13, 1967, to complete an earlier deal in which the Mets sent which pitcher to the Cardinals on July 16?

10 Al Jackson pitched a 1–0 shutout against St. Louis on October 2, 1964, to delay the Cardinal pennant clincher. Which St. Louis Hall of Fame pitcher did Jackson defeat?

11 On June 13, 1969, the Mets sold Al Jackson to what National League Western Division team where he finished his playing career?

12 Jackson had identical 8–20 won–lost records as a Met in which two seasons?

13 Jackson was the first Met pitcher to record five hundred career strikeouts. How many strikeouts did Jackson have as a Met?

14 While he was a member of the St. Louis Cardinals, Jackson allowed a grand slam to what Met pitcher on May 20, 1967?

15 What two uniform numbers did Jackson wear in his two tours of duty as a Met?

16 On May 4, 1965, Al fanned eleven Phillies in a 2–1 Met victory at Shea. That set a new record for most strikeouts in a game by a Met pitcher, erasing the old mark of ten. Which three pitchers held the previous record?

HOWARD JOHNSON

1 What is Howard Johnson's nickname?

2 When Johnson broke into the majors in 1982, who was his first manager?

3 Johnson hit his first major league home run on April 28, 1982, as a Detroit Tiger against Minnesota. This man who pitched for the Twins from 1976 to 1982 and had a 42–48 career record allowed the home run. Who is he?

4 How many seasons did Howard reach the "thirty home run–thirty stolen base club"?

5 In 1989, Johnson was tied for the league lead in runs scored with 104. Who were the other two National League players he was tied with?

6 What was Johnson's highest batting average as a New York Met?

7 Johnson became the second Met to hit home runs from both sides of the plate in one game when he did it on August 31, 1991, at Cincinnati. Who were the two Red pitchers that Howard "went yard" on?

8 In 1991, Howard led the National League in home runs and runs batted in. What were his season totals for both of those categories? (The RBIs were a club record.)

9 In 1991, Johnson became the first Met ever to lead the National League in runs batted in. What two National League players were tied for second place, an RBI behind?

10 Who had the old Met record of 108 RBIs, which was set in 1990?

11 What Met outfielder tied Johnson's RBI record in 1996?

12 Johnson has played in the most games at third base in Met history, with 835 games at "the hot corner." Three other Met third basemen have played in over five hundred games at third base. Name this trio.

13 Johnson had a pinch-hit grand slam home run on June 28, 1994, while playing for the Colorado Rockies. In the fourth inning, Johnson batted for Rockie pitcher Marcus Moore and connected for his seventh and final grand slam. The Padre pitcher who gave up Howard's blast also hurled for the Mariners, Rangers, and Cubs before ending his career in 1996. Name this right-handed pitcher.

14 Howard finished his major league career in 1995 with what team?

15 In 1987, Johnson set a National League record for most home runs in a season by a switch-hitter with thirty-six. Which St. Louis Cardinal first baseman held the old record of thirty-five homers in 1934?

CLEON JONES

1 Cleon Jones's major league debut was on September 14, 1963, as a defensive replacement. The center fielder Jones replaced was the first former Met to play for the Yankees. Can you name him?

2 Cleon smacked his first career home run on September 22, 1965, at Forbes Field in Pittsburgh. Who was the Bucco hurler who gave up Jones's first homer and became Cleon's teammate the following season?

3 Jones batted right-handed but threw left-handed, a rare occurrence for an outfielder. Name two other Met outfielders who also batted right and threw left. (One played for the Mets from 1987–1991, and the other was a Met in 1999 and part of the 2000 season.)

4 On May 14, 1969, Jones smacked his only career grand slam to highlight an eight-run eighth inning in a 9–3 Met victory. Which Atlanta Brave hurler, who later in his career was an important member of the 1973 National League Championship team, gave up the home run?

5 On July 18, 1969, after trying to score and being called out at home plate, Cleon got into a fight with a Montreal Expo catcher in a 5–2 Met win. Name the Expo backstop who also played with Pittsburgh and Houston.

6 Cleon set a team record by hitting .340 in 1969 and finished third in the National League batting race. Who were the two players who finished ahead of Jones?

7 What was the only other year that Jones hit over .300?

8 In 1970, Jones set a Met record for the longest consecutive game hitting streak (which has since been broken). How many games was Jones's streak?

9 Jones hit the thousandth home run in Met history on July 25, 1971, against the Houston Astros. Can you name the Astro pitcher who gave up the historic blast and who would throw a no-hitter for Houston in 1979?

10 Cleon hit into a triple play against the Astros on July 16, 1971. He became the fifth Met player to hit into a triple play. The previous time that a Met hit into one was on August 15, 1967, when a former Yankee did it against the Phillies. Name this harmonica-playing infielder.

11 On August 2, 1973, Cleon became the first Met to collect one thousand hits when he doubled against Pittsburgh. The Pirate pitcher who allowed this milestone hit once belted two home runs in a game for the Kansas City Royals on July 7, 1969. Can you name him?

12 In the fifth inning on July 20, 1974, Jones was one of three Mets to hit back-to-back-to-back home runs off San Diego pitcher Lowell Palmer. Who were the other two Mets who homered in that sequence?

13 How many home runs did Cleon Jones hit as a Met?

14 What American League team did Jones finish his major league career with in 1976?

15 Which Met had the previous record for highest batting average in a season (with at least 502 plate appearances) before Jones's 1969 season?

DAVE KINGMAN

1 What Pac-10 university did Kingman attend?

2 Kingman, as a member of the San Francisco Giants, smashed his first career home run on July 31, 1971, against a Pirate pitcher who led the National League in saves that season with thirty. Name this Bucco.

3 Kingman hit for the cycle and drove in six runs for the Giants against what team on April 16, 1972?

4 How many lifetime home runs did Kingman hit in his career?

5 He hit the most home runs (eight) off a Hall of Fame pitcher who had a twenty-four-year major league career. Can you name this hurler who retired in 1986 and was enshrined in 1994?

6 Kingman injured himself while playing left field on July 19, 1976, when he tore ligaments in his thumb on a ball hit by which Hall of Fame pitcher?

7 Kingman has the Met record for most multi–home run games in one season, which was set in 1976 with how many?

8 Kingman played on teams in all four divisions in 1977. Which two American League teams did he play for that season?

9 On July 28, 1979, Kingman hit three home runs in a game against the Mets. Which two Met pitchers did he homer against?

10 Kingman was reacquired by the Mets from the Cubs for what outfielder on February 28, 1981?

11 In 1982, Kingman became the first Met to lead the National League in home runs with how many?

12 What team did Kingman finish his playing career with?

13 In 1986, which was Kingman's final season, he set a major league record for the highest final season total of home runs in history. How many home runs did he smack?

14 While with the Cubs in 1979, Kingman led the National League in both slugging percentage (.613) and in home runs. How many home runs did he hit that year?

15 In 1979, Kingman also had his highest batting average of his career. What was his batting average that year?

16 Kingman's first major league manager played in the majors only one year (1942) with the New York Giants and caught just three games. In addition to managing the Giants, he served as an interim manager for both the 1976 Expos and the 1983 Cubs. Who is he?

17 Kingman belted six home runs at Shea Stadium as a visiting player in both 1979 and 1980, which ranks second in Shea Stadium history. This first-place slugger, who clubbed thirty-three home runs in 1968, hit seven home runs at Shea in 1968, a Shea Stadium record. Name him.

JERRY KOOSMAN

1 How many seasons did Koosman pitch for the Mets?

2 In 1968, Koosman finished fourth in the National League in earned run average. His ERA also set a Met rookie record, which still stands. What was Koosman's ERA in 1968?

3 In Koosman's rookie season, he tied a National League rookie record with seven shutouts. What Hall of Fame pitcher, who pitched in the National League for twenty years (1911–1930), also had seven shutouts in his rookie season?

4 Koosman became the first Met pitcher in their history to throw shutouts in two consecutive starts. It happened early in the 1968 season against which two teams?

5 Koosman hit two home runs during his major league career. His first was on September 18, 1968, against which Chicago Cub pitcher who went 16–10 in 1968?

6 Koosman holds the Met record for wins by a rookie with how many?

7 In 1968, Koosman finished second in the National League Rookie of the Year voting. What Hall of Famer finished first?

8 In a game at Jarry Park in Montreal on April 29, 1969, Koosman's left shoulder suddenly "popped," and he had to leave the game in a 2–0 Met victory. Can you name the Expo catcher who was at bat when Koosman was injured?

9 In the first game of a doubleheader at Shea Stadium on September 20, 1970, Koosman had a perfect game for the first five innings. This Pirate third baseman broke up the "perfecto" with a home run leading off the sixth inning. Who is this Pirate spoiler who began his big-league career with the San Francisco Giants in 1959?

10 What was the most batters Koosman ever struck out in a game?

11 Koosman registered his first career save on May 25, 1972, when he pitched the fourteenth inning at Wrigley Field, preserving a 3–2 Met victory over the Cubs. Who was the winning pitcher for the Mets in that game?

12 On July 22, 1975, Koosman stole his first career base in a game at Shea against the Cincinnati Reds when he stole second base in the third inning. Can you name both the Cincinnati pitcher and catcher whom Koosman stole against?

13 Koosman's 1976 season was his last winning season as a Met; he won twenty-one games (setting a Met record for left-handed pitchers) and struck out a career-high two hundred batters. However, he finished second in the National League Cy Young Award voting that year to a pitcher who would eventually pitch for the Mets. Can you name this pitcher?

14 Koosman was the starting pitcher for the Mets in the historic seven-hour, four-minute, twenty-five-inning game on September 11, 1974, against the St. Louis Cardinals at Shea. The Mets were leading 3–1 going into the ninth inning. With two outs and a runner on base, this Cardinal infielder homered off Koosman to tie the game and send it into extra innings. Who is he?

15 Koosman was also the starting pitcher on July 16, 1977, when the lights went out and the game against the Cubs was suspended. The game was resumed on September 16. The Cubs starting pitcher threw a complete game in a 5–2 Cub victory. Name this Cub pitcher who also pitched for the Mets in 1979 and 1980.

16 Koosman is third on the all-time Met list for career victories with 140. His last Met win occurred on July 13, 1978, when the Mets defeated the Reds 4–2 at Riverfront Stadium. Who was the losing pitcher for the Reds?

17 Koosman gave up Pete Rose's four thousandth career hit on April 13, 1984, as a member of the Philadelphia Phillies. Who was the Philadelphia manager on this historic day?

18 Who is the only other Met left-hander besides Koosman to win twenty games in a season?

ED KRANEPOOL

1 How many seasons did Ed Kranepool play for the Mets?

2 What New York City high school located in the Bronx did Kranepool attend?

3 Kranepool hit twenty-one home runs in three seasons at this high school to break the previous school record set by which first baseman and outfielder who was elected to the Hall of Fame in 1956?

4 How much money did Kranepool receive when he signed a bonus contract with the Mets in June of 1962?

5 Kranepool is the all-time Met career hit leader with 1,418. He got his first career hit (a double) on September 23, 1962, against a Chicago Cub pitcher who had 435 relief appearances, including one game with the Brooklyn Dodgers in 1957. Name him.

6 In 1966, Kranepool attained a career high in home runs. How many home runs did Kranepool hit that year?

7 In what year was Kranepool selected for the National League All-Star Team?

8 "Steady Eddie" was the first player to hit one hundred homers in a Met uniform. The hundredth came on August 3, 1976, against the Expos. Which Montreal pitcher, who later became a coach and subsequently an American League manager, allowed Kranepool's milestone blast?

9 How many career home runs did Kranepool hit?

10 On April 19, 1963, Kranepool slugged his first career home run. Name the Milwaukee Brave pitcher who gave up the home run and who later was a teammate of Kranepool in 1966 and 1967.

11 Kranepool holds the Met career record for pinch hits with how many?

12 What two seasons did Kranepool lead the National League in pinch-hit batting average?

13 Kranepool is the only Met first baseman to play in over one thousand games. How many games did Kranepool appear at the "initial sack"?

14 This Cub pitcher allowed Kranepool's thousandth career hit on May 12, 1974. Can you name this hurler who would later win a Cy Young Award in the 1980s?

15 On April 8, 1978, Kranepool appeared as a pinch hitter in the bottom of the ninth inning and smacked a two-run game-ending home run to defeat the Montreal Expos by a score of 6–5. What former Yankee Rookie of the Year served up the home run?

16 Kranepool slugged three pinch-hit home runs in 1978. For two of the homers, he batted for a pitcher who only had a one-year major league career. Name this pitcher who appeared in twenty-five games (all in relief) and had a 4–2 record.

17 "The Krane" is one of two players in team history who played at least ten years with the Mets and did *not* play for any other major league team. The other player was a catcher and was with the Mets from 1973 to 1984. Who is this backstop?

18 Kranepool participated in a triple play in the fourteenth inning in the second game of a doubleheader against San Francisco on May 31, 1964. Who was the Met shortstop who threw the ball to Kranepool to complete the triple play?

19 Eddie was seventeen years, ten months, and fourteen days old when he made his major league debut on September 22, 1962, thus becoming the youngest Met ever to make his major league debut. Which 1965 Met pitcher who at eighteen years, five months, and seven days was the second youngest in team history to make his big league debut?

AL LEITER

1 Leiter won his first career game in his major league debut on September 15, 1987, at Yankee Stadium in a 4–3 victory over Milwaukee. The losing pitcher for the Brewers hurled a no-hitter against the Orioles just four months earlier on April 15, 1987. Can you name him?

2 Leiter was traded by the Yankees to the Toronto Blue Jays on April 30, 1989, for what outfielder who led the American League in home runs in 1988?

3 Leiter hurled his first career shutout as a member of the Toronto Blue Jays, as he blanked the Boston Red Sox, 7–0, on June 17, 1993. Can you name the other two Blue Jays who played in that game who also played for the Mets at one time in their careers?

4 Al's career high for strikeouts in one season is two hundred. Which two seasons did he accomplish this?

5 Al threw the first no-hitter in Florida Marlins history when he defeated the Colorado Rockies, 11–0, on May 11, 1996. Whom did Leiter strike out to end the game?

6 Al started game 7 of the 1997 World Series for the Florida Marlins against the Cleveland Indians. He pitched six innings and did not figure in the decision. Who was the winning pitcher for the Marlins in that game, which went eleven innings with Florida winning, 3–2?

7 Which member of the 2000 Mets also pitched for Florida in the 1997 World Series with Leiter?

8 In Leiter's first season with the Mets (1998), he achieved a career high in victories with how many?

9 Leiter in 1998 became the first Met pitcher to hurl two shutouts in one season since which pitcher did it in 1993?

10 Al hurt his left knee and subsequently had to go on the disabled list when he went to cover first base in the seventh inning in a game against the Yankees on June 26, 1998. Which Yankee batter hit the grounder on the play that Leiter injured his knee?

11 Leiter recorded his thousandth career strikeout on June 12, 1999, when he defeated the Boston Red Sox, 4–2, at Shea. The batter who was number 1,000 played for the Mets in 1995 and is the son of a former Chicago White Sox and Baltimore Orioles player. Can you name this second-generation major leaguer?

12 What is Leiter's highest strikeout total in one game?

13 Leiter recorded his hundredth career victory on July 1, 2000, as the Mets defeated the Braves, 9–1, at Shea. Which Cy Young Award winner was the Braves losing pitcher that day?

14 Al won the Roberto Clemente Award in 2000. This award is given to the major league player who combines outstanding baseball skills with a sense of civic responsibility. What other New York Met won this award in 1989?

15 On April 20, 2001, Leiter gave up a grand slam home run to a Cincinnati Red who had not previously hit a grand slam in his major league career (6,734 at bats). Who is this veteran Red infielder?

16 Leiter pitched his fourth career shutout on May 23, 1998, as he blanked the Milwaukee Brewers on four hits as the Mets won, 3–0. Who made his Met debut in that game after being acquired from the Florida Marlins?

JON MATLACK

1 What is Jon Matlack's middle name?

2 Jon's first major league victory was on April 23, 1972, against the Chicago Cubs. The Mets were 8–2 winners. The Cubs losing pitcher in that game had a seventeen-year career and won 209 games in the big leagues with other stops in Baltimore, Cincinnati, and Atlanta. Name him.

3 On May 30, 1972, Jon raised his record to 6–0 with his first career complete game shutout as the Mets defeated the Phillies, 7–0. Which Hall of Fame pitcher took the loss?

4 On September 30, 1972, in his next-to-last start of his rookie season, Matlack gave up the three thousandth and final hit to a future Hall of Famer at Three Rivers Stadium. Who is this Pirate legend?

5 Matlack was awarded the National League Rookie of the Year Award in 1972. What Met finished third in the voting?

6 On May 18, 1973, Matlack suffered a hairline fracture of the skull when he was hit by a line drive by which Atlanta Brave infielder who played one game for the Yankees in 1977 before going to the Oakland A's?

7 Jon threw a one-hit shutout on July 10, 1973, as the Mets beat the Astros, 1–0. The only hit was a double by this Astro second baseman, who later managed for the Cincinnati Reds for parts of the 1988 and 1989 seasons. Name him.

8 Jon's career high in strikeouts was in 1973 with how many?

9 Jon is one of two Met pitchers to start three games of a World Series (1973). Who is the other pitcher?

10 On the day that Richard Nixon resigned as president of the United States, August 8, 1974, Matlack lost to the Pirates, 4–3, at Three Rivers Stadium on a home run in the ninth inning. Can you name this Pirate right fielder who was born in Brooklyn and ended the game with that homer?

11 In 1974, Matlack had an earned run average of 2.41 and finished third in the National League. A former teammate of Matlack's won the ERA crown with a 2.28 mark. Who is this former Met?

12 Jon led the National League in shutouts in 1974 with a club record-tying seven. What Hall of Fame pitcher finished second with six shutouts?

13 Matlack was tied with Jerry Koosman in 1976 for the team lead for most hits by a Met pitcher with how many?

14 How many games did Jon win as a Met?

15 What American League team hired Matlack to be a coach in 1996?

16 Matlack was 10–10 for the Texas Rangers in 1980. Who were the two members of the 1973 Mets who were Jon's teammates with the Rangers in 1980?

17 Matlack was the Mets' first-round draft choice and fourth pick overall in the June 1967 draft. The New York Yankees had the first selection that year and chose this first baseman/outfielder who became the first designated hitter in major league history. Can you name this player who made his debut in 1969, eight years after his bar mitzvah?

WILLIE MAYS

1 Willie hit his first major league home run on May 28, 1951, against a pitcher who was a Met for part of the 1965 season and Mays's teammate the remainder of 1965. Who is this Hall of Fame pitcher who Willie took "downtown" eighteen times?

2 What Negro League team did Willie play for from 1948 to 1950?

3 In Willie's rookie season, two men who played for the 1951 Giants later managed the Mets. Can you name this pair?

4 Mays won his only National League batting title in 1954 with a .345 batting average. Which New York Giant teammate of Mays finished second, hitting .342?

5 Mays led the National League in triples in 1957 with twenty. The next time a National Leaguer would have at least twenty triples would be thirty-nine years later in 1996. Ironically, it was a Met who accomplished this feat. Who is he?

6 Mays led the National League in stolen bases for four consecutive years. Name these years.

7 How many home runs did Willie Mays hit against the Mets?

8 Willie's highest run batted in total for one season was in 1962 with how many?

9 On May 26, 1962, Mays hit two home runs against the Mets at Candlestick Park. The second homer came with the Mets ahead, 6–5, with one runner on base and one out, and gave the Giants a 7–6 win. Which Met pitcher, who was 8–19 in 1962, yielded Mays's game-ending home run?

10 In 1962, Mays batted .304 and was part of an all-.300-hitting outfield. The other two outfielders later became major league managers. Can you name this duo?

11 Mays hit the six hundredth homer of his career on September 22, 1969, as a pinch hitter in the seventh inning and broke a 2–2 tie, as San Francisco defeated the Padres, 4–2. He became the second player in major league history to hit six hundred, and the historic homer came against Mike Corkins. Which future Met did he pinch-hit for?

12 Mays was traded to the Mets from the Giants on May 11, 1972. What pitcher did the Mets send to the Giants in the deal?

13 In his first game as a Met, Willie drove in the winning run when he homered in the fifth inning, breaking a 4–4 tie in a 5–4 Met win over the Giants. Which former Giant teammate did he homer against?

14 In his first game at Candlestick Park since becoming a Met, Mays on July 21, 1972, hit a two-run home run in the fifth inning, leading the Mets to a 3–1 victory over the Giants. It was Willie's 650th home run. What former University of Southern California star who led the Trojans to College World Series championships in 1968 and 1970 allowed this home run?

15 Mays was elected to the Baseball Hall of Fame in his first year of eligibility, becoming the fourteenth player to do so. It was also the first year that the Mets did not go over the one million mark in home attendance since Shea Stadium opened in 1964. Name that year.

16 What National League slugging outfielder who played with the Giants, Cubs, Dodgers, and Phillies from 1923 to 1934 was also inducted in the Hall of Fame the same year as Willie?

17 Mays is one of two players to play for both the New York Giants and the New York Mets. The other New York Giant/Met played for the Mets in 1966 and was acquired from the Boston Red Sox for outfielder Joe Christopher. Can you name this infielder who was the first pick of the Houston Colt 45's in the National League Expansion Draft on October 10, 1961?

18 On September 29, 1954, Mays made one of the great catches in World Series history when he robbed Vic Wertz of the Cleveland Indians of an extrabase hit. The base runners for the Indians were Al Rosen on first base and Larry Doby on second base, who advanced to third on the play. After the catch, Mays threw a strike to the Giant second baseman. Can you name this Giant "Keystoner"?

19 Willie Mays played under two managers during his tenure as a New York Giant. One of them was inducted in the Baseball Hall of Fame in 1994. The other managed the Giants two separate times and also managed the Angels and the Twins in an eighteen-year managerial career. Can you name this pair?

20 Mays had 187 home runs as a member of the New York Giants, which places him third on the all-time New York Giant list. Hall of Famer Mel Ott is first with 511 homers. This teammate of Willie who played the outfield and third base is second with 189 round-trippers. Can you name this two-term New York Giant who retired after the 1960 season and who also played with the Milwaukee Braves, Cubs, Red Sox, and Orioles?

21 Willie was the last active New York Giant when he retired after the 1973 season. The next-to-last active New York Giant began his career in 1952 and stayed with the Giants for five seasons before going to the Cardinals in 1957. Can you name this Hall of Fame pitcher who ended his career in 1972 with the Dodgers?

22 Mays returned from military service in grand style. In his first game back on April 13, 1954, he smacked a 425-foot home run in the bottom of the sixth inning. It was the final run scored in a 4–3 Giant triumph over the Dodgers at the Polo Grounds. The Brooklyn pitcher who allowed the homer won 122 games in a Dodger uniform from 1948 to 1959. Who is this Indiana-born right-hander?

23 Willie's third home run of the 1963 season (April 19) was the 371st home run of his career, and thus he passed Gil Hodges for the most home runs by a National League right-handed hitter. Can you name the Cub pitcher Willie homered against who had a 21–2 lifetime record against the Mets?

24 Who were the four San Francisco Giant Hall of Famers besides Willie who played in the famous twenty-three-inning game on May 31, 1964, at Shea Stadium?

25 In that same twenty-three-inning game, Mays was one of eight San Francisco players appearing in the game for the Giants who at one time during their major league careers played for the Mets. How many of the other seven can you name?

LEE MAZZILLI

1 Lee's dad Libero Mazzilli was a professional boxer. In which weight class did he box?

2 What is Lee Mazzilli's "cinematic" nickname?

3 What Brooklyn high school did Mazzilli attend?

4 As a youngster, Lee was a champion in what winter sport?

5 Mazzilli hit his first major league home run on September 8, 1976, in his second major league at bat, in Wrigley Field against a Cub pitcher who three years earlier appeared in all seven games against the Mets in the 1973 World Series. Can you name this southpaw who had a total of 143 career saves?

6 Mazzilli's initial major league home run was also a pinch hit. Which outfielder who had a five-year major league career, all with the Mets, did Lee bat for?

7 Mazzilli hit his second career home run on September 20, 1976. It came with two out and a runner (Leo Foster) on base in the bottom of the ninth inning and gave the Mets a 5–4 win over the Pirates, hurting Pittsburgh's chances of winning the National League East. The Pirate pitcher who gave up the homer, pitched in over one thousand major league games, all as a relief pitcher. Name him.

8 "Maz" belted a grand slam home run on July 4, 1978, for the only runs scored in a 4–0 victory over the Phillies in the first game of a twin bill. The pitcher who allowed the grand slam once hit two home runs against the Mets in one game. Who is this slugging pitcher?

9 Mazzilli became the first Met to hit home runs from both sides of the plate in the same game on September 3, 1978. Who were the two Dodger pitchers whom he homered against?

10 On July 23, 1979, on a ball hit by the Dodgers' Davey Lopes, Lee collided with another Met outfielder and was injured on the play. Mazzilli was hospitalized in Los Angeles and missed three games. Name the outfielder who was acquired by the Mets from the Cincinnati organization Mazzilli collided with.

11 On August 14, 1979, against Atlanta, Lee became the second Met to score five runs in a game. Who was the first Met to accomplish this feat, on May 18, 1978, also against the Braves?

12 Lee's best season was 1979. What was his batting average that year?

13 On July 15, 1980, in a 9–2 Met victory, Mazzilli homered in the ninth inning against the Braves in Atlanta. As he was crossing home plate, he got into a shouting match with an Atlanta Brave relief pitcher who threw at Met pitcher Pat Zachry earlier in the inning. Can you name this Brave reliever?

14 What was Lee's career high in stolen bases?

15 Mazzilli was traded to the Pirates from the Yankees on December 22, 1982, for four minor leaguers. One of those minor leaguers pitched for the Mets in 1991 and 1992. Who is he?

16 What American League team did Mazzilli finish his playing career with in 1989?

17 In 1986, Lee became the second player in World Series history to have a pinch hit from both sides of the plate in the same series. The first player to accomplish this feat did it for the 1918 Boston Red Sox against the Chicago Cubs. Can you name this switch-hitting catcher who played his entire career in the American League from 1913 to 1931 with five different teams, including the Yankees from 1921 to 1925?

18 On June 7, 1987, in the first game of a doubleheader at Shea against the Pirates, Lee hit a two-run double in the bottom of the ninth inning to give the Mets a come-from-behind victory. It was also Lee's thousandth major league hit. This former Pirate teammate of Lee's who gave up this milestone hit pitched for the Pirates from 1978 to 1987 before he was acquired by the Giants during the 1987 season. Who is he?

TUG MCGRAW

1 What is Tug McGraw's real first name?

2 McGraw was one of the more animated players in the major leagues. What mannerism did McGraw have while walking to and from the pitcher's mound?

3 Tug's first major league victory was in the second game of a doubleheader on August 22, 1965, as the Mets beat St. Louis, 4–2. Who was the Cardinal losing pitcher?

4 McGraw was the first Met pitcher to defeat Sandy Koufax. The Dodger Hall of Famer was 13–0 against the Mets when McGraw beat the Dodgers, 5–2, at Shea on August 26, 1965. Koufax would finish his career with a 17–2 lifetime mark against the Mets. Who was the other Met pitcher to beat Koufax just over a year later on August 30, 1966?

5 On April 27, 1969, in the second game of a doubleheader against the Chicago Cubs at Shea, McGraw was summoned from the bull pen with two men on base with no outs and a full count to Glenn Beckert. McGraw proceeded to retire Beckert, Billy Williams, and Ron Santo to preserve a scoreless tie. (McGraw would get credit for the victory in a 3–0 Met win.) The pitcher Tug replaced left the game because of a blister. Can you name this "hard luck" pitcher?

6 On April 7, 1970, the Mets defeated the Pirates, 5–3, at Forbes Field in Pittsburgh. This game marked the first time in their history that the Mets won an Opening Day game. McGraw registered the first of his ten saves that he would accumulate in 1970. Who was the winning pitcher for the Mets in that game?

7 What was McGraw's highest win total for one season?

8 Tug hit his only career home run on September 8, 1971, in Jarry Park against which Montreal Expo pitcher?

9 Tug had consecutive seasons with the same earned run average, 1.70. Which two seasons?

10 McGraw was the winning pitcher for the National League in the 1972 All-Star Game. Which Hall of Famer's single drove in the winning run the bottom of the tenth inning to give the NL a 4–3 victory and make McGraw a winning pitcher?

11 Tug's only career shutout took place on September 1, 1974, when he defeated Atlanta, 3–0. Who was the losing pitcher for the Braves?

12 McGraw was traded to the Philadelphia Phillies on December 3, 1974, with two other players for outfielder Del Unser, pitcher Mac Scarce, and minor league catcher John Stearns. Can you name the two outfielders who also went to Philadelphia along with McGraw?

13 At the time McGraw was traded, he was the all-time Met career save leader. How many saves did McGraw have as a Met?

14 McGraw was on the mound in game 6 when the Phillies won their first world championship in 1980. Which Kansas City Royal did McGraw strike out to end the World Series?

15 McGraw enlisted in the U.S. Marine Corps (USMC) toward the end of the 1965 season. One of Tug's Met teammates also enlisted in the USMC at the same time. Can you name this reliever who went 2–0 in 1965, his only season in the big leagues?

16 Tug retired from baseball after the 1984 season. Name the pitcher who was a Met from 1967 to 1978 who also was a Phillie teammate of Tug's in 1984.

17 Tug's "bread and butter" pitch was the screwball. He learned it in 1966 when he was in the Mets Florida Instructional League. Which former Yankee right-hander who led the American League in victories with twenty-three in 1962 taught McGraw "The Scroogie"?

18 Tug made his major league debut on Easter Sunday in the first game of a doubleheader against the San Francisco Giants on April 18, 1965. The first batter Tug faced struck out looking. Who was this Giant Hall of Famer?

FELIX MILLAN

1 Millan made his major league debut with the Atlanta Braves against San Francisco on June 2, 1966. In that game he collected his first major league hit, a single against this Giant hurler who also was the starting pitcher for the Giants in the famous twenty-three-inning marathon game against the Mets on May 31, 1964. Can you name this pitcher?

2 Millan hit his first career home run on September 28, 1967, against this Cincinnati pitcher who won twenty-two games for the Reds in 1965.

3 Millan hit his only career grand slam on April 9, 1969, against the Giants in a 10–2 Braves win. Which Hall of Fame hurler gave up Millan's grand slam homer?

4 On July 6, 1970, in a game against San Francisco, Millan had six hits in six at bats, including a double and a triple. He was the first National League player to go 6–6 since what Hall of Famer did it on July 8, 1965?

5 On May 1, 1971, with the score tied at 5–5 in the bottom of the ninth inning, Millan belted a two-run homer to give Atlanta a 7–5 win over the Los Angeles Dodgers. This Dodger pitcher, who has the same last name as a Brooklyn Hall of Fame pitcher, surrendered the home run. Can you name him?

6 Millan was acquired by the Mets on November 1, 1972, with pitcher George Stone. What two players went to Atlanta in that deal?

7 In what year did Millan play in all 162 games for the Mets?

8 In Millan's first season with the Mets, he set a team record with eighteen sacrifice hits in one year. The next season he rewrote the Met record book with twenty-four sacrifice hits, a record that still stands at the start of the 2003 season. This Met infielder held the previous mark of sixteen sacrifice hits in 1965. Who was this shortstop?

9 Millan on August 3, 1973, collected his thousandth career hit when he singled in the seventh inning. The St. Louis pitcher who allowed the hit had a son who played for the Mets in 1994 and 1995. Name both the father and the son.

10 In 1974, Millan set a Met record for the fewest strikeouts for one season with at least 502 at bats, a mark that still stands. How many times did Millan strike out that season?

11 Millan set a Met standard for most hits in a season with 191, breaking his own record of 185 set in 1973. Who eventually broke Millan's record for hits in 1996?

12 Who had the Met record for hits in one season before Millan broke the record in 1973?

13 In 1975, Millan set a club record with thirty-seven doubles. Who held the previous mark of thirty-six?

14 Millan drove in the only run in a 1–0 game at Shea against the Montreal Expos on April 10, 1976. In the fourth inning after Bud Harrelson tripled, Millan doubled to left field to score Harrelson. The Expo left fielder was later traded to the Mets in the 1980s. Can you name him?

15 On August 12, 1977, Millan injured his shoulder in a fight at Three Rivers Stadium. Name the Pittsburgh Pirate Millan tangled with who ended his Met playing career.

16 What Japanese team did the Mets sell Millan to on February 22, 1978?

JOHN OLERUD

1 John was drafted in the third round of the June 1989 free agent draft by the Toronto Blue Jays from what Pac-10 college?

2 John was the sixteenth player to make his professional debut in the major leagues since the inception of the free agent draft in 1965. What Hall of Fame player who was drafted in 1973 and never played in the minor leagues was the eighth player to make his professional debut in the major leagues?

3 Olerud smacked his first career home run on April 18, 1990, against the Baltimore Orioles. The pitcher who served up the home run would pitch for the Mets for three seasons and be Olerud's teammate in 1997. Name him.

4 John led the American League in doubles in 1993 with how many?

5 John also led the American League in batting average in 1993. What was his average?

6 Which pitcher did the Mets send to Toronto on December 20, 1996, to obtain Olerud?

7 John hit for the cycle for the Mets on September 11, 1997, against what team?

8 Olerud in 1998 became the second Met to record nine consecutive hits. The first Met to accomplish this feat did it in 1996. Name this Met infielder.

9 John set a Met record for highest batting average in one season in 1998, erasing Cleon Jones's old mark of .340. What was Olerud's batting average that season?

10 Olerud in 1998 became the first Met to finish in second place in the National League batting race. Which Met finished third in the 1990 National League batting race with a .328 average?

11 John played in at least 160 games for the Mets in 1998 and 1999. Who are the other two Mets who have played in at least 160 games in a season?

12 On June 16, 2001, Olerud hit for the cycle for a second time, this time as a member of the Seattle Mariners in the American League. Who was the first player to hit for the cycle in both leagues?

13 Olerud has a cousin who played in the major leagues from 1986 to 1999 with seven major league teams, including the Milwaukee Brewers, New York Yankees, and the Pittsburgh Pirates twice. Who is man who was the shortstop for the Brewers in 1987 and 1988?

14 Olerud shares the National League season record for most consecutive times reached base safely—fifteen times—with which five-time National League Most Valuable Player?

15 John led the Mets in runs batted in with 102 in 1997. Who is the Hall of Fame first baseman who led the Mets with one hundred RBIs in 1993?

16 On January 11, 1989, John was hospitalized after collapsing following an early-morning workout. He underwent surgery on February 27, 1989, for a brain aneurysm. Four years later, John was the recipient of the 1993 Hutch Award. This award goes to the major league player who best exemplifies the character, fighting spirit, and competitive desire of which former Tiger pitcher, who also managed Detroit along with the Cardinals and the Reds before he passed away from cancer in 1964?

17 John's dad (also named John) was drafted as a catcher in the fourth round of the June 1965 free agent draft. Which American League team drafted John Olerud Sr.?

REY ORDONEZ

1 From what country did Ordonez defect in 1993?

2 In his major league debut on April 1, 1996, against the St. Louis Cardinals, Rey collected his first hit, a single against a pitcher who had a twenty-one-year major league career with six teams including the Rangers and A's twice. Name this pitcher.

3 Rey also made a great defensive play in his first major league game. On a ball hit by Ray Lankford, left fielder Bernard Gilkey threw the ball to Ordonez, who was the relay man, and from his knees, Ordonez threw to the plate, where Todd Hundley tagged out the St. Louis base runner. Who was the Cardinal runner who was out at home?

4 Rey's longest consecutive batting streak took place during his rookie season. How many games did his hitting streak last?

5 Rey-o hit his first career home run on September 19, 1996, against the Phillies. Which Phillie rookie pitcher allowed Ordonez's first homer?

6 In 1997, Rey set a team record for position players for most consecutive at bats without a base hit. He surpassed the old record of thirty-four at bats, which was set by Don Zimmer in 1962 and later tied by Tommie Agee in 1968. How many at bats did Rey go hitless?

7 Rey won three consecutive National League Golden Glove Awards at shortstop from 1997 to 1999. Which active shortstop, who is playing in his eighteenth season in 2003 won the award from 1994 to 1996?

8 Ordonez holds the major league record for most consecutive errorless games by a shortstop, one hundred (June 14–October 4, 1999). What American League shortstop held the old major league mark with ninety-five games in 1990?

9 Rey hit his only career grand slam on September 18, 1999, against the Phillies. Which Philadelphia pitcher surrendered the home run?

10 Rey fractured his left arm in Los Angeles on May 30, 2000, while tagging out a Dodger base runner at second base. Name this Dodger who also played with Montreal and San Francisco.

11 During his Met career, Rey wore two uniform numbers. What are they?

12 On April 12, 2001, Ordonez's RBI single against Atlanta's Kerry Ligtenberg in the bottom of the tenth inning gave the Mets a 1–0 victory. Which Met scored the winning run?

13 Which two players did the Mets primarily use at shortstop after Ordonez was injured during the 2000 season?

14 Rey was the fourth Met to make his major league debut in the starting lineup for an Opening Day game. The first three times occurred in 1963, 1969, and 1979. Who are the other three players?

15 Rey started in seven consecutive Opening Day games for New York from 1996 to 2002. Who was the Met shortstop who was in the Opening Day lineup for both 1994 and 1995?

JESSE OROSCO

1 Jesse holds the major league record for most games pitched in relief, with 1,183 games through the 2002 season. Three other pitchers appeared in over one thousand games as *relief pitchers*. Can you name this trio?

2 In his All-Star debut in 1983, Jesse faced only one batter and struck him out. Which Milwaukee Brewer did he fan?

3 Orosco became the third Met relief pitcher to win both games of a doubleheader as the Mets swept the Pittsburgh Pirates at Shea by scores of 7–6 and 1–0 on July 31, 1983. Ironically, both games lasted twelve innings. The other two times it happened was on May 12, 1962, and August 23, 1964. Can you name the other two Met pitchers who accomplished this?

4 In that first game that Orosco won on July 31, 1983, the losing pitcher for the Pirates was a former Met farmhand who was a September call-up in 1969, but he never pitched for the Mets. Can you name this twelve-year veteran pitcher who threw a no-hitter for Texas in 1973?

5 On September 1, 1984, Jesse saved both games of a doubleheader against the Padres. Who were the two Met winning pitchers that day?

6 In 1984, Orosco had thirty-one saves, which at the time was a club record. Who had the old record of twenty-seven saves?

7 In a wild game against the Reds at Riverfront Stadium on July 22, 1986, Jesse alternated between pitching and playing right field. Another relief pitcher also alternated between the outfield and pitching in the same game. Who is the other relief pitcher?

8 Orosco, while playing right field in that game, even made a putout. Which Cincinnati Red Hall of Famer hit the ball that Orosco caught in right field?

9 Orosco was on the mound for the final out of the 1986 National League Championship Series. He struck out this Astro right fielder who later played for the Mets in 1992. Name him.

10 Jesse was also on the mound for the final out of the 1986 World Series. He struck out this Boston second baseman, who hit .433 in the series. Who was he?

11 On April 18, 1987, with the score tied at 8–8 in the bottom of the tenth inning in St. Louis, Orosco gave up a game-ending grand slam home run to a Cardinal infielder who later on would play for the Mets in 1990 and 1991. Who is this infielder who ended his career with the Giants, also in 1991?

12 What were the number of saves that Jesse collected in his Met career?

13 Jesse was reacquired by the Mets on December 10, 1999, for pitcher Chuck McElroy. However on March 18, 2000, he was traded to the St. Louis Cardinals for which infielder/outfielder?

14 Besides the Mets, Cardinals, and the two times he was with the Dodgers, what three American League teams did Orosco pitch for through the 2002 season?

15 Jesse garnered a total of ten base hits through the 2002 season. His first major league hit took place against St. Louis on September 10, 1982. The Cardinal pitcher who allowed Orosco's first hit had a twenty-five-year career, including a stint with the Yankees for part of the 1979 and 1980 seasons. Can you name him?

16 Jesse made his major league debut on April 5, 1979, facing and retiring the final batter in a 10–6 Met Opening Day victory over the Cubs at Wrigley Field. The lone batter whom Orosco faced in that game played against the Mets in the 1986 World Series. Who is he?

17 What Hall of Fame pitcher was on the losing end of Orosco's first major league victory on April 22, 1979?

MIKE PIAZZA

1 Piazza was drafted by the Los Angeles Dodgers in the June 1988 free agent draft in what round?

2 Piazza hit his first major league homer against the San Francisco Giants on September 12, 1992. The Giant relief pitcher who served up the homer led the National League in appearances in 1994 with sixty-one and later played for the Mets in the 2002 season. Who is he?

3 Mike became the regular Dodger catcher in 1993. Who was the regular Dodger catcher who caught over one hundred games in nine consecutive seasons from 1984 to 1992 and later managed a team that won a World Series?

4 Mike won the National League Rookie of the Year Award in 1993. Who was the last National League rookie catcher prior to Piazza to win this award in 1987?

5 Which future Met pitcher finished second to Piazza in the 1993 National League Rookie of the Year voting?

6 Mike was born in Norristown, Pennsylvania, on September 4, 1968. Which Hall of Famer who was inducted in Cooperstown in 1997 was also born in Norristown on September 22, 1927?

7 Piazza became the first player to homer in consecutive All-Star Games (1995 and 1996) since which Boston player did it for the American League in 1979 and 1980?

8 Mike's highest batting average for one season is .362. This occurred in 1997 and was the highest batting average for any National League catcher with one hundred or more games. What Hall of Fame catcher who spent his entire seventeen-year career in the American League hit .362 in 1936?

9 Mike was the second of five consecutive Dodger players to win the National League Rookie of the Year Award. Name the other four Dodgers who won this award in 1992, 1994, 1995, and 1996.

10 Mike's first hit as a Met came in his Met debut on May 23, 1998, and was an RBI double with two outs in the fifth inning against which Milwaukee Brewer pitcher who later appeared in two games for the Yankees in 1999?

11 On Piazza's first Met hit, which Met base runner scored from first base on the play?

12 Piazza's first home run as a Met came on June 1, 1998, against a Pirate pitcher who went 11–14 for the Buccos that season. Name him.

13 On April 14, 2000, Mike had a career high of five hits in one game. Against which team did he accomplish this?

14 Through the 2002 season, Mike has ended games with home runs five times in his career. In two of these games, he homered against the same pitcher. The first was on June 26, 1995, as a Dodger, and the second time was on April 28, 1999, as a Met. Who is this Padre pitcher whose brother was a major league manager?

15 Piazza became the seventh player in Met history to reach the "100 Home Run Club" when he homered in Philadelphia on September 22, 2000, against Randy Wolf. In fact, during the 2000 season, Mike passed four players who hit over ninety lifetime homers as Mets. Name this quartet.

16 Who is the only player who was a teammate of Piazza on the Dodgers, Marlins, and Mets?

17 What Hall of Famer who passed away in 2002 gave Piazza batting tips when Mike was twelve years old?

18 On June 17, 2001, in front of over fifty-four thousand fans at Shea, the Mets came back from a 7–2 deficit and scored six runs in the bottom of the eighth inning and defeated the New York Yankees by a score of 8–7. Piazza capped the rally by hitting a two-run homer against which Yankee relief pitcher who appeared in ten games for the Yankees in 2001?

19 While with Los Angeles, Mike caught a no-hitter in two consecutive seasons (1995 and 1996) by these two Dodger pitchers who were both born outside the United States. Name this pair.

20 Before Mike's Met debut on May 23, 1998, five different catchers started a total of forty-four games behind the plate for the Mets. Can you name this quintet of backstops?

21 On August 17, 2002, Piazza passed Johnny Bench for most home runs by a National League catcher when he slugged his 328th round-tripper as a backstop. The Dodger hurler who gave up the home run had a no-hitter for 6⅓ innings before Mike's homer broke up the potential pitching gem. Who is this Los Angeles southpaw?

22 On July 13, 2001, Mike became the ninetieth player in major league history to hit three hundred career home runs. He hit it off this Red Sox pitcher who would throw a no-hitter against Tampa Bay in 2002. Who is he?

23 On August 21, 2001, Mike hit his three hundredth home run as a catcher, becoming the fourth catcher to accomplish this feat. Can you name the Colorado Rockies pitcher who allowed this milestone homer, who pitched for the Mets in 2000?

24 The Mets were trailing 8–1, going into the bottom of the eighth inning in a game against the Braves on June 30, 2000. Remarkably, the Mets scored ten runs in the bottom of the eighth and went on to defeat Atlanta, 11–8. Piazza capped the scoring in that inning with a home run to put the Mets ahead to stay. The Brave pitcher who allowed the homer started his major league with San Francisco in 1986, the first of three separate stints with the Giants, and also pitched for the Yankees in 1994. Can you name this hurler who was active in 2002 with the Dodgers and Indians?

25 In the first regular season sporting event since the September 11, 2001 tragedy, the Mets beat the Braves, 3–2. Trailing 2–1 in the last of the eighth inning, Piazza hit a dramatic two-run homer against an Atlanta pitcher who was born in 1972 in Flushing, New York. Can you name this Queens native, who attended Christ the King High School and signed with the Yankees as a free agent on December 7, 2001?

RICK REED

1 Reed made his major league debut on August 8, 1988, against the Mets. He pitched eight innings and allowed three hits in a Pirate 1–0 victory at Three Rivers Stadium. Which two Mets accounted for the three New York hits?

2 What future Met drove in the only run in that game with a ground out in the fourth inning?

3 Rick was selected as the American Association Most Valuable Pitcher after going 14–4 in 1991 with which Pirate farm team?

4 Besides the Pirates, Mets, and Twins, Reed has pitched for three other teams through the 2002 season. Can you name them?

5 Fill in the blank: Rick Reed has been called "a poor man's _____." (Hint: A four-time Cy Young Award winner.)

6 Reed hit the first of his two major league homers on July 19, 1997, against the Cincinnati Reds. What former Met allowed Reed's first homer?

7 Reed hit his second career home run against the Cubs on April 15, 1998, against a pitcher who would pitch for the Mets starting in 2001. Who is this hurler?

8 What two seasons did Reed lead Met pitchers in base hits?

9 Reed was selected for the National League All-Star Team but did not pitch in which two years?

10 On June 8, 1998, Reed pitched his third career shutout as the Mets beat the Tampa Bay Devil Rays, 3–0. In that game, Reed retired the first twenty batters to face him until which future Hall of Famer broke up the perfect game with a double?

11 Eleven days later on June 19, 1998, Reed had a no-hitter until one out in the seventh inning against the Marlins. Which Florida World Series hero broke up Reed's no-hit bid?

12 On July 2, 1999, Reed played right field in the ninth inning in a 16–0 loss to Atlanta. Luis Lopez moved from second base to third base. Matt Franco moved from third base to pitch, replacing John Franco. What outfielder moved from right field to play second base so that Rick could play right field?

13 Reed pitched the first complete-game shutout for the Mets in 2001 when he blanked the Phillies, 9–0, at Veterans Stadium on June 5. The losing pitcher for the Phillies in that game hurled for the Mets in 1995 and 1996. Who is he?

14 When Rick made his major league debut in 1988, who was the Pittsburgh Pirate manager at the time?

15 Reed was traded from the Mets on July 30, 2001. Who was the outfielder the Mets received from the Minnesota Twins in the deal?

16 In 1998, Rick achieved a career high in victories. How many wins did Rick have that year?

17 From 1962 to 2002, there have been two other players in Met history who have the last name of Reed besides Rick. One was an outfielder who played for the Mets in 1990, and the other was a relief pitcher who was a Met for the last two months of 2002. Can you name this pair?

18 On October 2, 1999, Reed pitched a complete-game shutout over the Pirates, 7–0, at Shea to keep the Mets in the hunt for the National League wild card. It was his seventh career complete game and his fourth career shutout as he held the Buccos to three hits while striking out twelve. Which Pirate pitcher took the loss?

TOM SEAVER

1 What were the two notable nicknames Seaver had while pitching for the Mets?

2 Seaver was originally signed by the Braves in February 1966, but his contract was voided by the commissioner of baseball because the college that Seaver attended (University of Southern California) had already started the season when he signed. Who was the commissioner who made this ruling?

3 The commissioner ruled that any team wishing to match the Braves' offer could bid on Seaver. Who were the other two teams besides the Mets that put in a bid for Seaver in this special drawing?

4 Seaver spent 1966 pitching for Jacksonville, which was the Mets AAA affiliate in the International League. He had a 12–12 record and a 3.13 earned run average. His manager at Jacksonville played the infield for the Cardinals and Phillies from 1949 to 1959. Who is this former Cardinal manager?

5 What other Met pitcher is featured on Seaver's 1967 Topps rookie card?

6 Can you name the pitcher who was a teammate of Seaver at both Fresno High School in California and with the New York Mets?

7 This former New York Giant catcher from 1947 to 1957 was Tom Seaver's first major league manager. Name him.

8 Seaver's first major league win was on April 20, 1967, against the Cubs at Shea. The Mets won, 6–1, as Seaver went 7²/₃ innings. The losing pitcher for the Cubs in that game won 17 games for the 1950 National League Champion Phillies and had a twenty-year career winning 193 games. Who is he?

9 Seaver was the first member of the Mets to win the National League Rookie of the Year Award. Which St. Louis Cardinal pitcher finished second in the 1967 balloting?

10 Tom was the first National League pitcher to win Rookie of the Year since which Phillie pitcher, who had a 19–8 record, won the award in 1957?

11 On September 16, 1971, Seaver lost to the Cubs, 1–0, in a game at Shea. The only run in the game was a home run in the eighth inning by the opposing pitcher. Can you name the slugging pitcher who had a career total of eight home runs, including five with the Chicago White Sox?

12 In 1971, Seaver won twenty games, led the National League in strikeouts with 289 (a record for NL right-handed pitchers at the time), and also led in earned run average with a 1.76 mark. However, he finished second in the Cy Young Award voting. Who won the 1971 NL Cy Young Award?

13 In the strike-shortened 1981 season, Seaver led the National League in victories with fourteen and in winning percentage with .875. However, he finished second in the balloting and narrowly missed receiving the 1981 National League Cy Young Award by three points (70–67). Who won the 1981 NL Cy Young Award?

14 Seaver led the majors in wins in 1969 with a career high of twenty-five victories. Which pitcher inducted in the Hall of Fame in 1997 finished second in the National League in wins with twenty-three?

15 On October 1, 1974, Seaver tied the major league record of seven straight two hundred strikeout seasons. Which two Hall of Fame pitchers also had seven consecutive 200-K seasons?

16 In that same game in which the Mets lost to the Phillies, 3–1, Seaver fanned fourteen Phillies, including striking out the side in the ninth inning to run his total to 201. The two hundredth victim later played first base for the Mets in 1978 and 1979. Who is he?

17 On September 1, 1975, Seaver beat the Pittsburgh Pirates, 3–0, at Shea. It was his twentieth victory, and in that game, he became the first pitcher in major league history to fan two hundred or more batters eight consecutive seasons. Who was the Pirate batter that Seaver struck out in the seventh inning to set the record?

18 What were the three seasons that Seaver won the National League Cy Young Award?

19 While he pitched five one-hitters as a Met, Seaver did throw a no-hitter as a member of the Cincinnati Reds on June 16, 1978. Which St. Louis Cardinal outfielder made the last out of Seaver's gem?

20 This seven-year major leaguer who played for the Texas Rangers in addition to the Cincinnati Reds was Seaver's catcher when Tom no-hit the Cardinals. Can you name this backstop who hit two career home runs and had a lifetime batting average of .176?

21 As mentioned previously, Seaver hurled five one-hitters in a Met uniform: July 9, 1969, versus Chicago; May 15, 1970, versus Philadelphia; September 26, 1971, versus Pittsburgh; July 4, 1972, versus San Diego; and April 17, 1977, versus Chicago. Can you name the five batters who spoiled Tom's no-hit bids?

22 The previous Met pitcher to hurl a one-hitter before Seaver did it against the St. Louis Cardinals on May 4, 1966, as he allowed only a single in the third inning to future Met Ray Sadecki. Who is this pitcher who also played for the Phillies, Tigers, Angels, Indians, and White Sox?

23 On July 24, 1975, Seaver reached the two thousand strikeout plateau when he struck out this Cincinnati Red in the second inning in a game at Shea. Who is he?

24 How many times did Seaver lead the National League in strikeouts?

25 Seaver became the fifth pitcher in major league history to accumulate three thousand strikeouts on April 18, 1981, against the St. Louis Cardinals. Which future Mets star was Seaver's three thousandth victim?

26 Seaver was reacquired by the Mets from Cincinnati on December 16, 1982, for pitcher Charlie Puleo, outfielder Jason Felice, and a third player, who later became a major league manager. Can you name him?

27 Seaver made his return to the Mets on April 5, 1983, when he pitched on Opening Day against Steve Carlton and the Philadelphia Phillies. There were 48,682 fans in the stands to see the Mets blank the Phils, 2–0. Seaver, who did not figure in the decision, pitched six innings and left the game with a stiff left thigh muscle. Who was the winning pitcher for the Mets on that memorable day?

28 How many games did Seaver win as a Met?

29 Seaver won his three hundredth career game on August 4, 1985, as a member of the White Sox as Chicago beat the Yankees, 4–1, at Yankee Stadium. This future major league manager and future Met coach made the last out of the game for the Yankees. Name him.

30 The Yankee starting and losing pitcher in Seaver's three hundredth win would be a White Sox teammate of Tom's in 1986. Who is this pitcher who would throw a no-hitter for the Chisox in 1986?

31 This relief pitcher, who was the last of four hurlers used by the Yankees in Seaver's three hundredth win, was the only other former Met besides Seaver to appear in this historic game. Who is this man, who played for the Mets from 1979 to 1983?

32 In Seaver's final Met start on June 12, 1977, before he was traded to Cincinnati, Tom defeated the Houston Astros by a score of 3–1. The Houston batter who made the last out of the game eventually became manager of the Mets. Ironically, Dave Kingman, who was traded the same day as Seaver, caught the ball against the wall that ended this contest. Can you name the Astro infielder who was the final batter Seaver faced who ended his first Met career?

33 What year was Tom inducted into the New York Mets Hall of Fame and had his uniform number retired?

34 Tom was elected to the National Baseball Hall of Fame in 1992 with a pitcher whose career spanned from 1939 to 1955, compiling four twenty-win seasons and achieving consecutive American League Most Valuable Player Awards in 1944 and 1945. Who is this former Detroit Tiger and Cleveland Indian hurler?

---

35 Seaver made his major league debut on April 13, 1967, against Pittsburgh at Shea Stadium. Tom's mound opponent in his inaugural game pitched in the major leagues from 1966 to 1983 with the Pirates, Phillies, Tigers, Reds, and the Expos twice, winning 141 games. Who is this hurler who also was a tobacco farmer?

36 Seaver in his big league debut went 5⅔ innings, allowing six hits and two runs (both earned), walking four, and striking out eight. But he did not get credit for the victory. Can you name this former Baltimore pitcher who won eighteen games as an Oriole rookie in 1960 and made his Met debut in this game and was the winning pitcher?

37 Seaver smacked a total of six home runs as a Met. His first was on July 9, 1970, in a game against the Montreal Expos. The Expo pitcher who allowed Seaver's first homer also pitched for the Cubs and the Cardinals in a five-year career that began in 1966. Name him.

38 In his major league career, Seaver hit a total of twelve home runs. Tom's eleventh lifetime home run was hit against the Mets at Riverfront Stadium on June 4, 1979. The pitcher who gave up Tom's next-to-last homer won fourteen games for the Mets in 1979. Who is this pitcher who won fifty-nine games for the Mets from 1973 to 1984?

39 Tom "changed his socks" when he was traded from the Chicago White Sox to the Boston Red Sox on June 29, 1986. What outfielder/third baseman did Boston send to Chicago in that deal?

40 How many career strikeouts did Seaver have?

41 Tom won his 311th and final game on August 18, 1986. The losing pitcher in that game had a fifteen-year career, mostly in the American League. However, this man was on the mound for the Mets from 1989 to 1991. Who is this hurler who won at least twenty games in a season twice?

RUSTY STAUB

1 What is Rusty Staub's given first name?

2 What is Rusty's French nickname?

3 Rusty hit his first homer as a member of the Houston Colt 45's on June 3, 1963, against the Dodgers off which Hall of Fame pitcher?

4 On April 17, 1969, Rusty became the first Expo to get four extra-base hits in one game (three doubles and one home run), as the newly formed Montreal Expos defeated the Phillies at Connie Mack Stadium by a score of 7–0. The Expo pitcher that day threw a no-hitter in Montreal's ninth game. That pitcher went on to throw a second no-hitter on October 2, 1972, against the Mets. Who is he?

5 Staub was acquired by the Mets from the Montreal Expos on April 6, 1972. What three players went to Montreal in the deal?

6 In Staub's first game as a Met, he singled in his first at bat against the Pirates on April 15, 1972. The Pirate pitcher who allowed the hit pitched for the Mets for part of the 1979 season. Name him.

7 On the day that Willie Mays played his first game as a Met (May 14, 1972), Staub hit a grand slam in the first inning. Which Giant pitcher, who led the American League in strikeouts five times, allowed this grand slam?

8 On June 3, 1972, Staub got hit on the right wrist on a pitch thrown by an Atlanta Brave pitcher who would wind up being his Met teammate from 1973–1975. Who is he?

9 In game 4 of the National League Championship Series, with the game tied at 1–1 in the eleventh inning, the Reds had two runners on base and two out when a Cincinnati batter hit a long fly to deep right field. Rusty made a running one-hand catch before crashing into the wall, injuring his right shoulder. Name the Red player who hit the ball.

10 In 1983, Staub set a Met team record for consecutive pinch hits with how many?

11 On April 28, 1985, Rusty was inserted in the late innings and played the outfield for the first time since June 22, 1983, in an eighteen-inning game against the Pirates at Shea. In an interesting move by manager Davey Johnson, Staub flip-flopped between playing left field and right field, depending on the batter. Which Met outfielder also flip-flopped between left field and right field?

12 Rusty even had a putout in that game. Who was the Pirate batter who hit the fly ball that Rusty caught after a long run?

13 Rusty's last career home run (number 252) was hit on June 22, 1985, against the Montreal Expos. Batting for Lenny Dykstra in the seventh inning, Rusty hit a three-run homer to give New York the lead. The Expo pitcher who surrendered the home run pitched for the Mets from 1979 to 1981. Who is this pitcher who also pitched for the Red Sox and Yankees during his career?

14 In 1986, Rusty was one of the first two players inducted into the Mets Hall of Fame. Who was the other?

15 In what year did Rusty play for the Montreal Expos for the second time in his career?

16 Staub was traded to Detroit after the 1975 season. What pitcher who won three games in the 1968 World Series came to New York in that deal?

17 Rusty played for the Houston Colt 45's/Astros from 1963 to 1968. Three of his Houston teammates eventually were enshrined in the Baseball Hall of Fame in Cooperstown, New York. Can you name this trio?

JOHN STEARNS

1 What is Stearns's nickname?

2 Stearns was a standout in both baseball and football at what was then known as a Big Eight Conference school. It is presently in the Big Twelve Conference. Can you name this university?

3 What position did Stearns play as a college football player?

4 Stearns was the second pick in the June 1973 free agent draft. The Texas Rangers had the first selection and chose a pitcher who made his major league debut later that month. Who was this eighteen-year-old pitcher?

5 What National Football League team drafted John in the seventeenth round in the 1973 NFL draft?

6 On September 22, 1974, in the second game of a doubleheader between the Phillies and the Expos, Stearns pinch-hit for Tom Underwood and got a single for his first career hit. The Expo pitcher who yielded the hit pitched for the Mets in 1983 and 1984. Can you name him?

7 Stearns was traded by the Phillies with two other players to the Mets in December 1974 for Tug McGraw, Don Hahn, and Dave Schneck. What two players came to the Mets in addition to Stearns?

8 Stearns hit his first major league home run on April 30, 1975, against the Cubs. Name the Chicago pitcher who allowed the home run and pitched for both the Mets and Yankees in 1979.

9 On May 3, 1975, Stearns doubled in the fifth inning for the only hit that the Mets would get, as Montreal defeated the Mets, 3–0, at Shea. The Expo pitcher who hurled the one-hitter threw another one-hitter against the Mets in 1966. Who is he?

10 In a game against the Los Angeles Dodgers on August 10, 1975, one of Stearns's return throws accidentally hit a pitcher in the eye. This right-handed pitcher had just come in the game to relieve Rick Baldwin. As a result, he sustained a ruptured vessel in the right eye and was subsequently put on the disabled list. Who is this pitcher?

11 On June 30, 1978, the Mets beat the Pirates at Three Rivers Stadium by a score of 6–5. On the last play of the game, Dave Parker was thrown out attempting to score. Stearns received the throw from right fielder Joel Youngblood and held on to the ball after a collision, while Parker wound up with a broken cheekbone. The Pirate batter who hit the ball became a Met coach after he retired as an active player. Who is he?

12 In 1978, Stearns set a record for National League catchers with twenty-five stolen bases. Which Chicago Cub catcher had twenty-four stolen bases in 1902 for the previous mark?

13 That record for most stolen bases by a National League catcher lasted until 1998, when a Pirate catcher swiped twenty-six bases. Can you name this Pittsburgh backstop?

14 On July 26, 1980, Stearns fractured his right index finger when he was hit by a foul tip by which Cincinnati Red infielder?

15 What two years did Stearns serve as a coach for the Mets?

16 Stearns's last year as a player with the Mets was 1984. Who were the other four catchers who played for the Mets that season?

DARRYL STRAWBERRY

1 The Los Angeles high school that Darryl graduated from also produced the NBA's Marques Johnson, the NFL's Wendell Tyler, and third baseman Chris Brown, who played with the San Francisco Giants from 1984 to 1987. Can you name this high school?

2 Darryl was the number one pick in the country in the June 1980 draft. The Mets had an additional first-round pick in 1980. Can you name this outfielder who played with the Mets in 1984 and 1985 and later became a major league general manager?

3 Who was Darryl's first major league manager?

4 Darryl picked up his first major league hit (an RBI single) in the eighth inning on May 8, 1983, against the Cincinnati Reds in New York. Which Cincinnati reliever allowed the hit?

5 "Strawman" connected for his first career homer on May 16, 1983, against the Pirates. Who was the opposing pitcher?

6 What was Darryl's highest batting average for one season?

7 In 1987, Darryl and which other Met became the first set of teammates to reach the "Thirty Home Run–Thirty Stolen Base Club" in the same season?

8 Darryl became the all-time Met leader in home runs on May 13, 1988, as he hit his 155th home run, passing Dave Kingman. Strawberry broke the record against an Atlanta Brave pitcher who spent his first five years with San Diego before pitching with the Indians in 1983. Who was that pitcher?

9 What was the only season that Strawberry led the National League in home runs?

10 There have been six times in Darryl's career that he has ended games with a home run. Two of the homers have been against the same pitcher. Name this pitcher, who was with Cincinnati from 1984 to 1989 and was a teammate of Darryl in 1990.

11 How many home runs did Strawberry hit in a Met uniform?

12 When Darryl played for the Dodgers, one of his boyhood friends was a teammate of his during 1992 and 1993. Who is this outfielder?

13 Who is the only other player besides Darryl to play for the Mets, Yankees, Dodgers, and Giants?

14 On October 1, 1985, Strawberry hit a monster home run in St. Louis in the eleventh inning to give the Mets a 1–0 win and put them just two games behind the Cardinals, with five games left to play. Who was the Cardinal pitcher who yielded the home run?

15 On July 28, 1996, Strawberry hit a game-ending two-run home run in the bottom of the ninth inning to give the Yankees a 3–2 win over the Royals. It was Darryl's three hundredth career homer. The Kansas City relief pitcher who gave up the homer hurled for the Mets in 1994 and 1995 as a starting pitcher. Can you name him?

16 On May 11, 1985, Darryl tore a ligament in his right thumb when he made a diving catch of a sinking line drive in the third inning of a Mets' 4–0 win over the Phillies. He was placed on the disabled list and was activated on June 28. The Phillie batter who hit the ball subsequently played for the Mets in 1989. Who is he?

CRAIG SWAN

1 What Pac-10 college did Swan attend?

2 Craig got his first major league win on May 11, 1974, at Wrigley Field in a 6–3 Met triumph over the Cubs. The entire Met outfield that day each hit home runs in support of Swan. Name this trio of outfielders.

3 Swan was the opposing starting pitcher when this San Francisco Giant pitcher threw a no-hitter against the Mets on August 24, 1975. Name him.

4 Swan hurled his first complete-game shutout on April 28, 1976, when he defeated the Atlanta Braves, 3–0. The losing pitcher for the Braves in that game won twenty games for the California Angels and Los Angeles Dodgers three years apart. Who is he?

5 Swan only allowed one grand slam homer in his Met career, and it came in the fifth inning against the St. Louis Cardinals on May 28, 1976, in a 6–0 Cardinal victory at Shea. The Cardinal who hit the grand slam played with the Dodgers the previous twelve years and then finished his career in 1977 with the Astros and A's.

6 Swan led the National League in earned run average with a 2.43 mark in 1978. This Expo narrowly finished second with an ERA of 2.47. Can you name this right-handed hurler who spent his entire career in Montreal from 1973 to 1985?

7 On July 25, 1978, Swan gave up a single in a third inning to this man who in this particular game set a new National League record for most consecutive games with a base hit surpassing Tommy Holmes's record of thirty-seven games. Name him.

8 Craig hooked up with Gaylord Perry in a pitching duel on July 20, 1979, at San Diego. With the score tied at 1–1, Swan gave up a home run to the Padre left fielder in the bottom of the ninth inning and lost 2–1. Name this Padre left fielder who had a total of forty-five homers in his ten-year career.

9 On April 26, 1981, Swan allowed a single to Montreal leadoff hitter Tim Raines to start the game. The next hitter was Jerry Manuel; on the first pitch, Raines stole second, but the throw from the catcher hit Swan and resulted in a fractured rib and a stay on the disabled list. Name the Met catcher.

10 Swan belted his only career home run on August 4, 1982, against which Hall of Fame pitcher who was enshrined in 1991?

11 How many career wins did Swan have as a Met?

12 Craig garnered his first career save on July 18, 1979, against the Dodgers for which winning pitcher who was a Met rookie in 1979?

13 What American League team did Swan finish his career with in 1984?

14 What two seasons did Craig win ten or more games for the Mets?

15 Swan made his major league debut on September 3, 1973, in the second game of the Labor Day doubleheader. He was the losing pitcher in a 6–3 defeat to the Phillies. The Philadelphia starting pitcher in that game made his professional baseball debut in the major leagues a few months earlier on April 17, 1973, after being selected in the January 1973 draft. Who is this right-hander?

RON SWOBODA

1 What Atlantic Coast Conference college did Ron Swoboda attend?

2 On April 14, 1965, Swoboda in his second major league at bat collected his first career hit. It was a pinch home run. Who was the Houston pitcher who gave up Swoboda's initial homer?

3 How many home runs did Swoboda hit in his rookie season?

4 What was Swoboda's highest batting average for a season?

5 What was Swoboda's nickname?

6 On April 30, 1965, Swoboda came to bat in the first inning with the bases loaded and hit a fly ball that hit the wall and fell back to the playing field. The Mets contended that the ball went over the home run line for a grand slam, but second base umpire Frank Secory disagreed, and Swoboda got credit for a single. In which park (now defunct) did this controversial play take place?

7 On August 4, 1968, in the second game of a doubleheader at Dodger Stadium, Swoboda got the only hit (a single in the seventh inning) by the Mets in a 2–0 loss to the Dodgers. Can you name this pitcher who threw the one-hitter who also hurled for the Yankees from 1969 to 1973?

8 In a game on September 13, 1969, the Mets beat Pittsburgh, 5–2, at Forbes Field, extending their winning streak to ten games. Swoboda's first career grand slam was the key to victory. Which Pirate hurler allowed Swoboda's blast?

9 In game 4 of the 1969 World Series, Swoboda made one of the most incredible catches in World Series history. Who was the Baltimore Oriole Hall of Famer whom Swoboda robbed of a hit?

10 In game 5 of the 1969 World Series, Swoboda broke a 3–3 tie with a run-scoring double in the eighth inning that gave the Mets a 4–3 lead. The Mets would win the game, 5–3, and take their first world championship. Who scored the run for the Mets on Swoboda's two-base hit?

11 Swoboda's tenure with the Mets ended on March 31, 1971, when he was traded to the Montreal Expos along with minor league infielder Rich Hacker. Who was the outfielder the Mets received from the Expos?

12 When Swoboda was traded, he was the all-time Met leader in home runs. How many home runs did Swoboda hit during his six-year Met career?

13 With what team did Swoboda finish his major league career?

14 A total of fifty-three pitchers allowed home runs to Swoboda. Which Hall of Fame pitcher allowed the most home runs (four) to Ron?

15 Ron's first year in professional baseball was in 1964. He spent time between Buffalo (International League) and Williamsport (Eastern League). Both of Ron's managers that year were teammates on the 1942 world championship St. Louis Cardinals. The skipper of Buffalo was a third baseman and batted .254, while the manager of Williamsport went 7–5 with two saves in 1942. Can you name this pair?

ROBIN VENTURA

1 Ventura had a fifty-eight-game hitting streak as a sophomore and appeared in the College World Series in 1986 and 1987. What university, currently in the Big Twelve Conference, did he attend?

2 The hitting streak was stopped during the 1987 College World Series against Stanford by this pitcher who would later be Robin's teammate with the White Sox from 1990 to 1994. Name him.

3 Robin was on the gold medal–winning United States Olympic Baseball Team in 1988, hitting .409. In what city did the Summer Olympics take place that year?

4 Robin garnered his first major league hit on September 12, 1989, against Baltimore and his thousandth career hit on August 17, 1996, against Milwaukee. Ironically, it was against the same pitcher. Can you name this pitcher who was Robin's Olympic teammate?

5 Ventura hit his first career home run on April 18, 1990, against a pitcher who has recorded over three thousand strikeouts. Name this pitcher.

6 What Hall of Fame pitcher did Ventura tangle with on August 4, 1993, when he charged the mound after being hit by a pitch, which resulted in a two-game suspension?

7 In 1993, Robin became the first American League third baseman to record at least three consecutive seasons with ninety or more RBIs since this Yankee, who did it from 1975 to 1978?

8 Robin hit two grand slams in one game on September 4, 1995, and became the eighth player in major league history to accomplish that feat. What Hall of Famer was the seventh player to do it, on June 26, 1970?

9 On June 6, 1996, Robin participated in a 5-4-3 triple play for the White Sox. Who were the Chicago second baseman and first baseman involved in the play?

10 Robin won five Golden Glove Awards for the White Sox. Only two third basemen in American League history have won more. Name this pair.

11 Robin began his Met career by hitting safely in his first ten games to open the 1999 season. Prior to Ventura, the last time a Met opened the season with a ten-game hitting streak was in 1991 by this Met catcher who was only with them for one season but played on the Yankees three separate times. Who was he?

12 On May 20, 1999, Robin became the first player in major league history to hit grand slams in each game of a doubleheader. Name the two Milwaukee pitchers who were victimized.

13 Ventura belted his two hundredth career homer on September 1, 1999, against what Houston Astro pitcher who went 5–13 in 1999?

14 When Ventura was traded from the Mets to the Yankees on December 7, 2001, which outfielder did the Mets get in return?

15 Including the 2002 season, Ventura has 275 lifetime homers. How many career grand slams does he have?

16 From 1962 to 2002, there have been seventy-three players who have played for both the Mets and Yankees. Four players were added to that list in 2002. Robin was one of those four. Who are the remaining three?

17 Robin hit five grand slams as a Met and is tied for second place with three other Mets on the Mets all-time list. Can you name the trio with whom Robin is tied?

18 Robin's first major league manager also piloted the Mets in 1992 and 1993, along with being a coach for the Yankees from 1979 to 1988. Who is this former catcher who began his managerial career with the Cleveland Indians in 1977?

MOOKIE WILSON

1 What is Mookie's real first name?

2 What Southeastern Conference university did Mookie lead to the NCAA Atlantic Region Championship and second place in the College World Series in 1977?

3 Mookie collected his first career hit on September 4, 1980, at San Diego. The Padre pitcher who gave up the hit was a fifteen-year veteran who also toiled for the Red Sox, Cardinals, Giants, and Angels from 1970 to 1984. Who is this left-hander?

4 Mookie smacked his first career home run on June 2, 1981, against the Phillies. Which former Met surrendered the homer?

5 What year did Mookie have at least ten doubles, ten triples, ten home runs, and ten stolen bases?

6 On April 28, 1985, Mookie scored the winning run in the bottom of the eighteenth inning as the Mets defeated the Pirates, 5–4, in a five-hour, twenty-one-minute marathon. Which backup catcher/outfielder delivered the winning hit?

7 Who was the Met base runner who scored the winning run on Mookie's ground ball that eluded Red Sox first baseman Bill Buckner in the tenth inning of game 6 in the 1986 World Series?

8 In the game in which Dwight Gooden returned after his drug rehab (June 5, 1987), Mookie made a remarkable catch in left field after colliding and butting heads with center fielder Lenny Dykstra. Which Pirate first baseman hit the ball?

9 Mookie collected his thousandth career hit on July 22, 1988, against an Atlanta Brave pitcher who signed with the Mets as a free agent after the 2002 season. Who is he?

10 Mookie is the all-time Met leader in steals with how many?

11 Mookie also is the all-time Met leader in triples with how many?

12 On September 20, 1981, Mookie came up with Frank Taveras on second base and two outs when he smacked a game-ending home run to defeat the Cardinals, 7–6. The Cardinal pitcher who yielded Mookie's homer led the National League in saves that year with twenty-five. Who is this relief specialist?

13 With what American League East team did Mookie finish his playing career in 1991?

14 What year was Mookie elected to the Mets' Hall of Fame?

15 Mookie made his major league debut at Dodger Stadium on September 2, 1980, in a 6–5 Met loss. Mookie went hitless in four at bats and played center field. Who were the other two Met outfielders who played in that game?

16 Mookie smacked two home runs in one game only once in his career. This took place in Philadelphia on April 10, 1988. Mookie hit both homers off the same hurler who pitched for the Yankees from 1982 until June 30, 1984, when he was traded to the Phillies for pitcher Marty Bystrom and outfielder Keith Hughes. Who is this left-hander who began as a Seattle Mariner in 1978?

17 Mookie was the Opening Day center fielder for the Mets from 1982 to 1985, 1987, and 1989. Who started for the Mets in center field on Opening Day 1990, which was a 12–3 loss to the Pirates at Shea?

18 Wilson hit sixty-seven career homers (sixty as a Met) against fifty-five different pitchers. The most he hit against any pitcher was three, against a pitcher who played for the Padres, Expos, and Angels from 1980 to 1987. Who is this hurler who led the National League in appearances with fifty-seven games in 1981?

METS TRIVIA:
The Managers

YOGI BERRA

1 Who was the Yankee manager when Yogi made his major league debut on September 22, 1946?

2 Yogi hit 358 lifetime home runs. The pitcher he homered the most against yielded eleven home runs to him. Name this four-decade pitcher who was inducted into the Baseball Hall of Fame the same year (1972) that Yogi was.

3 Yogi caught two no-hitters during the 1951 season by one Yankee pitcher. Can you name him?

4 Two of Berra's boyhood friends from St. Louis became major lea-guers and were teammates on the New York Giants for part of the 1954 season. Can you name this pair?

5 Berra hit his ninth and final grand slam on June 23, 1962. The Tiger pitcher who allowed the home run also pitched for the White Sox and Dodgers and was a member of the Chicago Cubs from 1968 to 1972. Can you name him?

6 Berra hit eight home runs in his final season as an active player with the Yankees. He smacked his 358th and final homer on September 21, 1963, in the fourth inning with Joe Pepitone on base against the Kansas City A's. The pitcher who served up the home run would be a World Series hero three years later. Who is he?

7 Who replaced Berra as manager of the New York Yankees after the 1964 season?

8 On May 1, 1965, Berra made his Met debut as an active player when he came up as a pinch hitter in the eighth inning in a 9–2 loss to Cincinnati. He grounded out to Reds first baseman Gordy Coleman. Which Met pitcher did Berra bat for?

9 On May 4, 1965, Berra recorded two singles in a 2–1 Met victory. His two hits (the last two of his career) were against two different Phillie pitchers. Name this pair.

10 In the same game, Berra scored the winning run in the seventh inning. Which Met infielder drove in the run that scored Berra?

11 On May 9, 1965, Berra played his last major league game. He was hitless in four trips to the plate against a pitcher who later would coach for the New York Yankees. Can you name this Milwaukee pitcher?

12 There have been seventy-three players who have played for both the Mets and the Yankees from 1962 to 2002. However, only four of them did *not* play for any other major league team. Berra is one of them. Who are the other three?

13 Berra's first game as Met manager was on April 15, 1972, a 4–0 win over Pittsburgh at Shea. What Met drove in three of the runs with a two-run homer and a sacrifice fly?

14 Berra played on fourteen pennant-winning teams and has the record for most hits in World Series play with how many?

15 Yogi was the second manager in major league history to win pennants in both the American League and National League. This former Cub/Yankee skipper was the first. Name him.

16 As of April 1, 2003, Berra is the second-oldest living former Met. Berra was born on May 12, 1925. The oldest living former Met is Warren Spahn, who was born on April 23, 1921. What former Brooklyn Dodger, born on August 6, 1926, is the third oldest former Met?

17 What National League team did Yogi coach from 1986 to 1989?

18 In 1950, Yogi caught in 148 games. Aside from manager Casey Stengel and coach Bill Dickey, four of Yogi's teammates from 1950 also were enshrined in the Baseball Hall of Fame. Can you name this quartet?

19 On October 4, 1955, in the final game of the 1955 World Series, Yogi hit an opposite-field fly ball that was caught by the Brooklyn left fielder who relayed the ball to the shortstop, who in turn threw to the Brooklyn first baseman to complete a double play that killed a possible Yankee rally. Who were the three Dodgers that participated in this "twin killing"?

20 Who was the Yankee base runner who was "erased" on this play?

21 In 1984, Yogi became manager of the New York Yankees for the second time. Two players on the 1984 Yankee team later became major league managers themselves. Can you name this pair?

22 Yogi is one of five men who played, coached, and managed for the Mets. Who are the other four?

23 What three seasons did Yogi receive the American League Most Valuable Player Award?

24 Berra made his major league debut on September 22, 1946, in the first game of a doubleheader against the Philadelphia Athletics at Yankee Stadium. He had two hits in four at bats, including his first major league home run against Jesse Flores. The starting pitcher Yogi caught in that game recorded his nineteenth victory en route to a 20–8 season. Can you name this eleven-year veteran who pitched for the Yankees during his entire career?

25 Also making his major league debut in the same game as Berra was this Yankee infielder who played for the Yankees from 1946 to 1954. This man later became the American League president from 1984 to 1994, in addition to becoming a physician. Who is he?

26 When Yogi became the Met manager in 1972, who became the Met first base coach?

GIL HODGES

1 Gil made his major league debut on October 3, 1943, and played third base. Who was the Brooklyn Dodger manager at the time of Gil's debut?

2 Gil hit his first major league home run on June 18, 1947, at Wrigley Field against a pitcher who two years earlier had won at least ten games each for both the Yankees and Cubs. Name him.

3 In 1947, Hodges was a backup catcher for the Brooklyn Dodgers as he was an understudy for Bruce Edwards. What other former major league manager caught for Brooklyn in 1947?

4 On May 17, 1947, Hodges garnered his first hit in the major leagues when he came up as a pinch hitter for pitcher Harry Taylor and delivered a single against Pittsburgh in a game at Forbes Field. The Pirate pitcher who surrendered the hit pitched fifteen years in the big leagues, starting his career with the Red Sox in 1934, before pitching with the Browns from 1941 to 1943. Can you name this southpaw who also hurled for Brooklyn in 1943 and 1944?

5 On June 14, 1947, in the second game of a day–night doubleheader at Sportsman's Park in St. Louis, Gil started his first game in the majors as a catcher. (Gil went hitless in four at bats against Harry Brecheen.) The Dodger starting pitcher in that game spent his entire six-year career with Brooklyn, including hurling a no-hitter against the New York Giants on September 9, 1948. Later on he became the public address announcer for the Baltimore Orioles. Who is he?

6 On August 31, 1950, the Dodgers slaughtered the Boston Braves, 19–3, as Hodges became the first "modern" National League player to homer four times in a nine-inning game. Hodges homered off four different pitchers. Warren Spahn, Normie Roy, and Bob Hall were the first three hurlers to allow homers to Gil. The fourth homer came in the eighth inning and was against a pitcher who also pitched for the New York Giants from 1954 to 1957 and was purchased by the Mets on October 11, 1961, from the Milwaukee Braves but decided to retire before 1962. Can you name this two-time twenty-game winner?

7 Which Brooklyn outfielder who was a Dodger from 1946 to 1960 was on base for all four of Gil's home runs?

8 How many consecutive years did Gil drive in one hundred or more runs with the Brooklyn Dodgers?

9 Gil hit the Mets' first home run in their history in the fourth inning of their first game on April 11, 1962. Which Cardinal pitcher did he hit it against?

10 On May 16, 1962, in a game at the Polo Grounds, Hodges smacked his only career inside-the-park home run. It was a solo shot and happened in the eighth inning against the Cubs, tying the game at 5–5. The Chicago pitcher who allowed the home run lost twenty games for the Cubs in 1962 before winning twenty-two the following season. Who is this Cub southpaw?

11 Hodges participated in the first Met triple play, which Willie Davis of Los Angeles hit into during the second game of a doubleheader on May 30, 1962. Who were the Met shortstop and second baseman who also took part?

12 When Hodges hit his 370th and final home run on July 6, 1962, he passed Ralph Kiner for tenth place on the all-time home run list. The Cardinal pitcher who gave up the homer was a twenty-game winner for St. Louis in 1964 and had two tours of duty with the Mets. Who is he?

13 On May 5, 1963, in the second game of a doubleheader at the Polo Grounds against the San Francisco Giants, Gil recorded his 1,291st and last hit when he singled in the fourth inning against a Giant pitcher who appeared against the Los Angeles Dodgers in the 1959 World Series as a member of the Chicago White Sox. Who is this pitcher, who won 211 games in the majors from 1945 to 1964?

14 On that same play, Gil also drove home a former Brooklyn teammate en route to a 4–2 Met victory. Name this infielder.

15 Gil became the manager of the Washington Senators on May 22, 1963. The man who started the 1963 season as the Washington manager played in the majors from 1939 to 1960. Can you name this fourdecade player?

16 Hodges managed his first game for the Washington Senators on May 23, 1963. The Senators lost to Baltimore, 6–0. What Hall of Fame pitcher threw a two-hit shutout, spoiling Hodges's managerial debut?

17 In what was to be Hodges's final game as Met manager, the Mets beat the Cardinals, 6–1, as Tom Seaver won his twentieth game and rewrote his record of most strikeouts in a season by a National League right-hander, with 289. It was also to be the last game in a Met uniform of a player who hit two home runs in that game. Can you name this outfielder who was traded shortly before the 1972 regular season?

18 In Hodges's first game as manager of the Mets, New York had a 4–2 lead going into the bottom of the ninth inning but lost to San Francisco, 5–4, as the Giants scored three runs to rally and win the game. The loss was New York's seventh consecutive Opening Day setback. Can you name the Giant outfielder whose double drove in the tying and winning runs? He later played for the Mets in 1975.

19 This outfielder who played twelve years in the majors managed the Senators in 1968 after Gil left to manage the Mets. Can you name this "fly chaser" who played for the Indians, Senators, Twins, Phillies, and White Sox?

20 When Hodges came over to manage the Mets in 1968, he took three of his coaches from Washington with him. Can you name this trio?

21 In 1955, the Brooklyn Dodgers captured their only world championship, and Gil played a major part in the final game. The Dodgers won game 7 by defeating the New York Yankees, 2–0, as Gil drove in both runs. Name the two Dodgers who are enshrined in the Hall of Fame who scored the only two runs of the game.

22 Hodges handled the final putout of game 7. Can you name the Yankee batter who was a rookie in 1955 and stayed with them for thirteen years who grounded out to the shortstop to end the 1955 series?

23 Hodges became the fifteenth player in major league history to reach the three hundred home run plateau when he homered against the Cubs' Dick Drott in the seventh inning on April 23, 1958, in a game won by the Cubs, 7–6. What National League outfielder who finished his career in 1944 and was a Phillie three separate times, and who was enshrined in the Baseball Hall of Fame in 1980, finished his career with three hundred homers?

24 Gil won three consecutive Golden Glove Awards from 1957 to 1959. Who was the National League first baseman who won the award for seven consecutive seasons, from 1960 to 1966?

25 During his tenure as the Met "skipper," Hodges managed three players who were once teammates of Gil, as either a Met or a Dodger. Can you name this trio?

DAVEY JOHNSON

1 Johnson was the Orioles' regular second baseman from 1966 to 1972. Who played second for Baltimore on a regular basis from 1961 to 1965?

2 Johnson hit his first major league home run on April 26, 1966. The California Angel pitcher who allowed the homer tied for the American League lead in shutouts in 1967. Can you name this pitcher, who passed away at the age of thirty-two?

3 Johnson was one of four Baltimore Orioles to hit a home run in the seventh inning against the Red Sox in a 12–8 Baltimore victory on May 17, 1967. Who were the other three Orioles to homer in that inning?

4 Davey hit his first career grand slam on June 5, 1968, against the California Angels. The pitcher who gave up the home run has a son who made his major league debut in 1997 with Cleveland. Can you name this Angel pitcher?

5 Davey won three consecutive Golden Glove Awards for American League second basemen. Which three years did he accomplish this?

6 On December 30, 1972, Johnson was traded to the Atlanta Braves with three other players for catcher Earl Williams and infielder Taylor Duncan. Two of the players who went to Atlanta were pitchers Pat Dobson and Roric Harrison. The other player who went with Johnson to the Braves eventually became a major league manager. Who is this former backstop who also caught for the Yankees in 1980 and 1981?

7 Johnson broke a 3–3 tie against the Mets on May 8, 1973, when he belted a grand slam in the top of the seventh inning against a Met relief pitcher who replaced Jon Matlack after he was struck in the head by a line drive. Name him.

8 On September 8, 1973, Johnson won a game for the Braves with a home run in the bottom of the ninth to defeat Cincinnati, 3–2. The losing pitcher for the Reds in that game pitched for the Mets in 1975 and 1976. Who is he?

9 In 1973, Johnson hit forty-three homers. As a second baseman, he hit forty-two homers, which tied the major league record set in 1922 by which Hall of Fame Cardinal, who also was a Met coach in 1962?

10 Who were the two other members of the Atlanta Braves who hit at least forty homers in 1973?

11 When Johnson became manager of the Mets in 1984, whom did he replace?

12 Davey garnered his 340th victory as Met manager, breaking Gil Hodges's previous club record of 339 as the Mets won the second game of a doubleheader against the Braves, 5–1, on July 7, 1987. (The Mets also won the opener, 6–2.) Which Met reliever picked up his first career save in Davey's milestone game?

13 Johnson has won the most games as Met manager with how many?

14 Besides the Mets and Orioles, what two other major league teams has Davey managed?

15 Who became the new Met manager when Davey was fired in 1990?

16 Davey made his major league debut with Baltimore on April 13, 1965. His first major league manager played the outfield for the Yankees from 1948 to 1959, before being dealt to the Kansas City Athletics as part of a six-player trade that brought Roger Maris to the Bronx Bombers. Who is this man, who also managed the A's, both in Kansas City and in Oakland?

17 In Johnson's major league debut, which was against the White Sox, he came up as a pinch hitter against Chicago's Gary Peters and struck out. This Orioles pitcher that Davey batted for pitched for Baltimore from 1960 to 1967 before being traded to the Yankees for first baseman Ray Barker and two minor leaguers. Who is this fifteen-year veteran?

18 Davey recorded his first major league hit on April 22, 1965, when he pinch-hit for Orioles pitcher Wally Bunker. The Senator pitcher who allowed Davey's first hit had a 39–47 mark for Washington from 1962 to 1970, as both a starter and a reliever. Who is he?

19 During his tenure at Baltimore, Johnson teamed up with one of the best defensive shortstops in major league history. Can you name this eight-time Golden Glove Award winner, who passed away in 1998?

20 Davey slugged 136 career home runs during his thirteen-year major league career. The most home runs he hit off one pitcher was six, against a pitcher who either won or shared two consecutive Cy Young Awards in the 1960s. Who is this controversial hurler?

21 While a member of the Philadelphia Phillies, Davey slugged two pinch-hit grand slams in one season (1978), thus becoming the first pinch hitter in major league history to accomplish this feat. On April 30, he batted for pitcher Randy Lerch and homered against a San Diego pitcher who would eventually pitch for the Yankees from 1983 to 1987. Can you name this southpaw?

22 Davey's second pinch grand slam of 1978 took place on June 3, when he homered against the Dodgers' Terry Forster. The Phillie player he batted for would be traded a week later to the Yankees with outfielder Bobby Brown for pitcher Rawley Eastwick. Can you name this "clubhouse jokester" who played in the big leagues from 1966 to 1985?

23 What National League team was Davey traded to for pitcher Larry Anderson on August 6, 1978, where he finished his major league playing career?

24 Davey finished in a tie for third place in the 1966 American League Rookie of the Year Award with George Scott of the Boston Red Sox. Which future Met won the award that year in the AL?

25 Davey became the first skipper in National League history to win at least ninety games in each of his first five years as a manager. Which Hall of Fame "pilot" was the first to accomplish the same feat in the American League from 1951 to 1955 as manager of the Cleveland Indians?

CASEY STENGEL

1 Stengel hit sixty homers in fourteen National League seasons from 1912 to 1925. What was his highest season total?

2 Stengel sported his highest batting average over a full season hitting .316 in 1914 while playing right field for Brooklyn. In fact, he was part of an all-.300-hitting outfield. Who were the other two members of this Dodger outfield who batted over .300?

3 In 1914, Stengel led the National League in on-base percentage with a .404 clip. This New York Giant was second with .403. Who was this Giant left fielder who also led the National League in runs scored that season?

4 On July 17, 1917, while with Brooklyn, Stengel smacked a solo home run in the bottom of the tenth inning to give the Dodgers a 2–1 victory over St. Louis. The pitcher who yielded the homer lost twenty games for the Cardinals that season. Who was he?

5 Stengel hit the first World Series home run in Yankee Stadium history, in game 1 of the 1923 "Fall Classic." In the top of the ninth inning, with the score tied 4–4, Stengel hit an inside-the-park homer to give the Giants a 5–4 victory. What Yankee pitcher gave up Casey's winning dinger?

6 That inside-the-park home run that Casey hit in the 1923 World Series was only the second inside-the-park home run in World Series history. The first one was hit in game 2 of the 1916 World Series by one of Casey's teammates against Babe Ruth of the Red Sox. Can you name this Brooklyn outfielder?

7 On November 12, 1923, Stengel was traded from the New York Giants to the Boston Braves. What other Hall of Famer went from the Giants to the Braves in that trade and became a player-manager for Boston?

8 Stengel made the last out of a no-hitter by grounding out to St. Louis second baseman Rogers Hornsby on July 17, 1924. Name the Cardinal pitcher who threw the no-hitter and was inducted into the Hall of Fame in 1970.

9 Brooklyn was the first major league team that Casey managed for. What years did he pilot the Dodgers?

10 Casey managed the New York Yankees from 1949 to 1960. In those twelve seasons, the Yankees won ten American League pennants and seven World Series titles. Name the three seasons that Stengel's Yankee teams lost to the National League representatives in the World Series (ironically, all in seven games).

11 Which other Yankee manager besides Casey also won seven World Series titles?

12 Who preceded Stengel as Yankee manager in 1947 and 1948?

13 Who succeeded Stengel as Yankee manager in 1961?

14 Who took Stengel's place as manager of the Mets after Casey broke his hip on July 24, 1965?

15 How many games did Stengel win as Met manager?

16 Who is the only player that Casey managed both as a Boston Brave and as a New York Met?

17 Casey managed his last game for the Mets on July 24, 1965, at Shea. The Mets lost to the Phillies, 5–1, as Jim Bunning struck out twelve and held the Mets to two hits. What Met outfielder got both hits that Bunning allowed, including a home run in the fourth inning for the Mets' only run?

18 Stengel was inducted into the Baseball Hall of Fame in 1966. What slugging American League outfielder was enshrined along with Casey?

19 This pitcher, who retired after the 1984 season, was the last active player to play for Stengel. Who is he?

20 This man was mainly a shortstop with four National League teams from 1891 to 1911 and was Casey's first major league manager. Can you name this former infielder who, while with the New York Giants, led the NL in runs batted in with eighty in 1904?

21 On July 30, 1964, a pregame celebration was held at Shea Stadium for Stengel's seventy-fourth birthday. Six Dodgers—including Willie Davis, future Hall of Famer Don Drysdale, and Maury Wills—emerged from the visiting dugout and did a parody of the song "The Band Played On." One of the other Dodgers who sang was a $125,000 selection by the Mets in the October 10, 1961, expansion draft, but he never actually played a game for the Mets. Who is this outfielder, who also played for the Pirates, Cubs, Reds, and Phillies?

22 Five men played under Casey while they were both members of the Mets and members of the Yankees. Can you name this quintet?

23 What are Casey's given first and middle names?

24 Casey made his major league debut on September 17, 1912, with Brooklyn, against the Pittsburgh Pirates at Washington Park. Brooklyn won the game, 7–3, and ended the Pirates' twelve-game winning streak. Stengel contributed four hits, reached base on a walk, and stole two bases. He got his first hit off a pitcher who led the Federal League in victories with twenty-nine in 1914 while pitching for the Chicago Whales. Name this pitcher.

25 Since 1900, Casey is one of three members of the Baseball Hall of Fame to have four hits in his major league debut. Who are the other two? (One debuted in 1959 and the other in 1984.)

JOE TORRE

1 Which catcher did Milwaukee trade to the San Francisco Giants in December 1963, enabling Torre to become the Braves' first-string catcher?

2 Torre belted his first home run on May 21, 1961, against the Cincinnati Reds. The pitcher who yielded the home run won twenty-one games for the National League pennant winning Reds that year. Name him.

3 Torre finished second in the 1961 National League Rookie of the Year voting to what future Hall of Fame player?

4 In 1965, Torre was part of a Milwaukee Brave team that had six players with twenty or more home runs. In addition to Torre, who had twenty-seven, there were two Hall of Famers, Hank Aaron and Eddie Mathews, who had thirty-two apiece. Who were the other three?

5 How many career home runs did Torre hit against the Mets from 1962 to 1974?

6 One of those homers took place on May 17, 1967, when Torre hit a game-ending home run to give the Braves a 4–3 victory. Name the Met rookie pitcher who allowed the home run.

7 On March 17, 1969, Torre was traded from the Atlanta Braves to the St. Louis Cardinals for which future Hall of Famer?

8 When the Mets clinched the National League Eastern Division in 1969, Torre was the last Cardinal batter of the game. He grounded into a double play. Who were the three Met fielders who took part in that double play?

9 When Torre won the National League MVP in 1971, how many base hits did he have?

10 In his first game as a Met on April 8, 1975, Torre's RBI single in the bottom of the ninth inning gave the Mets a 2–1 win over the Phillies and Steve Carlton on Opening Day. Who scored the winning run for the Mets?

11 From 1996 through 2002, Torre as a manager has won nineteen games in World Series competition, which is sixth place on the all-time list. The other five managers ahead of Torre are enshrined in the Baseball Hall of Fame. Can you name this quintet?

12 On April 13, 1977, Torre hit his 252nd and last career home run. It was a pinch home run and came in the ninth inning against Clay Carroll in a 7–3 loss to the Cardinals. Which Met relief pitcher did Torre hit for?

13 Torre was a player-manager for the Mets until he took himself off the active roster on June 18, 1977. He was the first player-manager in the National League since 1959 when the Cardinals had one. Can you name this double-duty Cardinal who also was a Met coach during the Polo Grounds years?

14 Torre is the fourth man to manage both the Mets and the Yankees. Who are the other three?

15 In 1964, Torre hit .321, with 20 homers and 109 runs batted in, to become the first catcher since 1955 to hit .300 with at least 20 homers and 100 RBIs. Which Hall of Fame catcher accomplished this feat in 1955?

16 Before Torre became the St. Louis Cardinal manager for the final fifty-eight games of the 1990 season, he was a television announcer for what American League team from 1985 to 1990?

17 Who were the two Cardinal managers in 1990 prior to Torre's hiring?

18 Who did Joe replace as Met manager on May 31, 1977?

19 Joe made his big league debut on September 25, 1960. His first manager was the skipper of five major league teams, including a stint with the Brooklyn Dodgers from 1951 to 1953. Can you name this man, who died in 1966 after starting the season as manager of Detroit?

20 Torre hit the first regular season home run in Atlanta–Fulton County Stadium on April 12, 1966, against a Pirate pitcher who went 16–12 for Pittsburgh in 1966. Can you name this Bucco leftie?

21 Which former two-term Met player replaced Torre as interim Cardinal manager on June 16, 1995?

22 On September 25, 1960, Joe made his major league debut a successful one when he came up as pinch hitter for Warren Spahn and singled. The Pittsburgh pitcher who yielded Torre's first hit won 136 games over a fourteen-year major league career that included stops for the Cardinals, Phillies, Reds, and Orioles. He was also the Mets' pitching coach in 1966 and 1967. Name this diminutive southpaw.

23 When Torre retired in 1977, his 252 career home runs were the fifth most of any player born in the state of New York. Name the four sluggers who were at the top of this list.

24 This pitcher, who won twenty or more games in six different seasons and was inducted into the Baseball Hall of Fame in 1983, allowed eight home runs to Torre, the most of any pitcher whom Torre homered against. Who is he?

25 In addition to Henry Aaron, Eddie Mathews, and Warren Spahn, Torre was a teammate of six other players who are currently in the Baseball Hall of Fame and were enshrined as players. How many can you name?

BOBBY VALENTINE

1 In 1970, Valentine led the Pacific Coast League with a .340 batting average. What team did he play for?

2 What Hall of Fame manager was the skipper of that team?

3 Valentine hit his first major league home run as a member of the Los Angeles Dodgers on June 13, 1971, against the Expos at Jarry Park. The Montreal pitcher who gave up the home run was a former Met farmhand and was included in a significant trade in Met history. Name this pitcher who played from 1969 to 1983.

4 On May 17, 1973, Bobby broke his right leg when he ran into the center field wall at Anaheim Stadium while chasing a home run by an Oakland player. Who is this A's infielder?

5 What was Valentine's highest batting average in a season in which he played over one hundred games?

6 On June 15, 1977, Valentine was traded by the San Diego Padres to the Mets along with a pitcher for Dave Kingman. Name this pitcher whose dad played for the Dodgers, Cardinals, and Athletics in the 1930s and 1940s.

7 Bobby hit his twelfth and final home run on May 4, 1978, against what Hall of Fame pitcher?

8 What team did Valentine finish his playing career with in 1979?

9 Whom did Valentine replace as manager of the Texas Rangers in 1985?

10 Who replaced Valentine as manager of the Rangers starting with the 1993 season?

11 When Valentine left the Mets to manage the Texas Rangers, who became the Met third base coach?

12 In 1995, Valentine became the first American manager to pilot a Japanese team. What team in the Japanese Pacific League did Valentine manage?

13 Valentine became the sixteenth manager in Met history on August 26, 1996. Whom did he replace as manager?

14 Bobby has the second-most career wins as Mets manager, trailing only Davey Johnson. How many victories does Bobby have as a Met manager?

15 Bobby was a first-round pick in the June 1968 draft as the Dodgers had the fifth selection overall. The Mets had the first pick in the 1968 draft. The shortstop whom the Mets selected had two tours of duty with the Mets. Can you name this Californian who was a teammate of Bobby in 1978?

16 Bobby made his major league debut on September 2, 1969—ironically, against the Mets, when he appeared as a pinch runner. Valentine scored on a single by Andy Kosco in the ninth inning as the Mets held on to win 5–4, with the Dodgers scoring three runs in the bottom of the ninth to make it close. Which Dodger infielder did Valentine pinch-run for?

17 While subbing for regular shortstop Maury Wills, Valentine collected his first major league hit on April 25, 1971, in the first game of a doubleheader against the Cincinnati Reds. This Cincinnati pitcher who allowed the hit had a sixteen-year major league career and also pitched for the Indians, Cubs, Tigers, and Mariners before retiring after the 1986 season. Name him.

18 Valentine was traded from the Dodgers to the Angels on November 28, 1972. What Hall of Famer also went from LA to Anaheim in the deal?

19 For what National League West team did Valentine coach third base in 1993?

20 Valentine and Joe Torre were opposing managers in the 2000 World Series. Twenty-three years earlier—June 17, 1977—marked the only time that they appeared in the same game as Met teammates and both appeared as pinch hitters in a 7–1 loss to the Houston Astros. The pitcher Valentine batted for made his Met debut in this game. Can you name this former Red, who also hurled for the Dodgers and Phillies?

21 Valentine and Torre are two of six men who managed in the major leagues in 2002 who at one time played for the Mets during their major league careers. Can you name the other four?

22 On May 20, 1972, in a game at Dodger Stadium against the Houston Astros, for the only time in his major league career, Bobby led off the first inning with a home run. He homered against a pitcher who subsequently ended his career with the Mets in 1981. Can you name this left-hander who in 1971, while as a San Diego Padre, had the second-lowest earned run average (2.10) in the National League, behind Tom Seaver's 1.76?

23 On July 14, 2001, Valentine became the forty-eighth manager in major league history to register one thousand victories as the Mets defeated the Boston Red Sox, 2–0. The Met starting pitcher in that game hurled eight innings and allowed only one hit, a two-out bunt single in the first inning to Trot Nixon, while striking out ten. Who is this southpaw who was traded to the Brewers on January 21, 2002?

24 Bobby's father-in-law pitched for the Brooklyn Dodgers from 1944 to 1953 and again for one game in 1956. Who is this man who was involved in one of the most famous moments in baseball history?

25 On April 18, 1978, Bobby came off the bench and delivered the big hit, a two-run double against the Cardinals' Eric Rasmussen in the seventh inning, as the Mets defeated the Cardinals, 3–2. Valentine pinch-hit for the starting pitcher, who recorded his first major league win. Can you name this Jamaica, Queens, native who only pitched in the majors in 1978?

POSTSEASON YEARS

1969

1 On Opening Day of the 1969 season, the Mets lost to the Montreal Expos, 11–10, who were playing their first game in their history. The Expo winning pitcher in their debut pitched for the Mets in 1967 and 1968. Name him.

2 On April 27 in the second game of a doubleheader at Shea, Cleon Jones broke up a scoreless game in the bottom of the ninth inning by hitting a three-run homer and giving the Mets a 3–0 win over the Chicago Cubs. Name the Cub pitcher who allowed Jones's game-ending blast.

3 What infielder's RBI single in the eleventh inning gave the Mets a 1–0 victory on May 28 and started the team's eleven-game winning streak?

4 Which Hall of Fame pitcher ended the Mets' eleven-game winning streak on June 11 with a 7–2 victory?

5 In what could be described as the first "important" regular season game in their history on July 8, 1969, the Mets scored three runs in the bottom of the ninth and defeated the Cubs, 4–3. Ed Kranepool drove in the winning run with a single. Name the Hall of Fame pitcher who allowed Kranepool's game-winning hit.

6 On August 13, the Mets lost 8–2 to the Houston Astros, completing a three-game series sweep by the Astros. It was after this game that the Mets went 38–11 to win the National League Eastern Division. How many games behind the Cubs were the Mets after August 13?

7 On September 10, the Mets reached first place for the first time in their history when they beat the Montreal Expos at Shea, 3–2, in twelve innings. Who got the winning single off Expo relief pitcher Bill Stoneman that scored Cleon Jones to give the Mets the victory?

8 On September 12, the Mets beat the Pirates in a doubleheader at Forbes Field. Each game was 1–0, and the Met pitcher drove in the only run in both contests. Who were the two Met pitchers?

9 On September 15, the Mets beat the Cardinals, 4–3, in St. Louis. This Cardinal pitcher fanned nineteen Mets but gave up a pair of two-run homers to Ron Swoboda and was the losing pitcher. Name this Hall of Fame pitcher.

10 The Mets were held hitless on September 20 by Bob Moose as the Pirates beat the Mets, 4–0. The Met who made the final out of the no-hitter was the only other Met besides Cleon Jones to hit .300 in 1969. Who was he?

11 What rookie pitcher hurled a four-hit shutout when the Mets clinched the National League Eastern Division crown on September 24?

12 In that division-clinching game, the Mets won, 6–0. All the Met runs were scored as the result of home runs. Who were the two Mets who homered in the game?

13 What Atlanta Brave outfielder who started the season with the expansion San Diego Padres made the last out in the third and final game of the 1969 National League Championship Series (NLCS)?

14 Three players who participated for the Atlanta Braves in the 1969 NLCS played for the Mets in the 1970s. Name this trio.

15 Who drove in the winning run in the Mets' first-ever World Series victory?

16 Tommie Agee made two of the greatest catches in World Series history in game 3 of the 1969 World Series. Who were the two Oriole batters who were denied hits due to Agee's heroics?

17 Which Baltimore Oriole pitcher gave up Ed Kranepool's only World Series home run?

18 Davey Johnson made the last out of the 1969 World Series when he flied out to Cleon Jones. Who was the on-deck batter for the Orioles when the World Series ended?

19 Of the twenty-one Met players who participated in the 1969 World Series, only one had prior World Series experience. Can you name him?

20 Who were the four Met pitchers who were eligible to play in the 1969 World Series but did not?

21 Which infielder, who appeared in forty-nine games at third base and in eleven games at second base and who had five pinch hits in nine pinch-hit at bats, was left off the Mets' postseason roster?

22 This hurler was the starting pitcher in the first game in Montreal Expo history against the Mets at Shea on April 8, 1969. He also appeared in relief in the Mets' Eastern Division clincher at Shea for the St. Louis Cardinals on September 24. Who is this pitcher who homered in the 1965 World Series?

23 Who was the home plate umpire who awarded Cleon Jones first base when Jones was hit by Orioles pitcher Dave McNally in the sixth inning of game 5? (He umpired in the American League from 1963 to 1980.)

1973

1 On Opening Day 1973 (April 6), the Mets beat the Phillies, 3–0. Cleon Jones contributed to the Met win by hitting two home runs. What Hall of Fame pitcher gave up the two homers to Jones?

2 Tug McGraw popularized the slogan for the 1973 season in the Mets' march to the World Series that year. What was this famous rallying cry?

3 What Met rookie broke up a no-hit bid by Atlanta's Ron Schueler with a single in the ninth inning on July 6 in a 2–0 Brave victory?

4 In a game on July 7, Atlanta's Ralph Garr hit an inside-the-park home run on a play where the Met left fielder suffered a dislocated right hip as he collided with the center fielder. Who were the two Met outfielders who ran into each other?

5 On August 17, Willie Mays hit his 660th and final home run against what Cincinnati pitcher, who later became a coach for the Reds?

6 On September 2, in a 7–4 Met loss at St. Louis, Felix Millan was involved in a brawl with a member of the Cardinals that resulted in both benches emptying. Name this Cardinal, who later became a successful broadcaster.

7 On September 20, one of the most miraculous fielding plays in Met history took place. In the top of the thirteenth inning, Pittsburgh's Dave Augustine hit a long fly ball that hit the top of the left field wall, bounced straight up, and landed in Cleon Jones's glove. Jones fired the ball to the relay man, who in turn hurled the ball to the catcher, nailing Richie Zisk at the plate to preserve a 3–3 tie. Name the Met relay man and the catcher.

8 On September 21, the Mets reached first place in the National League East. They reached the .500 mark (77–77) for the first time since May 29. What was the largest amount of games that the Mets were behind the first place team in 1973?

9 Which Met had four hits (all singles) in the Eastern Division clincher against the Cubs at Wrigley Field on October 1?

10 What Cub was the final batter in the game when the Mets clinched the 1973 Eastern Division Crown?

11 In game 2 of the 1973 National League Championship Series, the Mets won, 5–0, and evened the series at one game apiece. Jon Matlack pitched a two-hit shutout for New York. Which Red outfielder who played with the Yankees in 1968 collected both hits?

12 In game 3 of the 1973 NLCS, Rusty Staub belted a pair of home runs, leading the Mets to a 9–2 victory. Which two Cincinnati pitchers did Staub homer against?

13 In addition to the fight between Bud Harrelson and Pete Rose in game 3, there was another fight between a Met pitcher and a Cincinnati Red pitcher. Name the two principals in this brawl.

14 In the first game of the 1973 World Series, the Oakland A's won 2–1 as Felix Millan's error paved the way for two unearned runs in the third inning. Who was the Oakland batter who hit the ball that skipped between Millan's legs?

15 In the 1973 World Series, Tug McGraw appeared in five games with a 1–0 record and one save. His save took place in game 5, preserving a 2–0 win for Jerry Koosman. Can you name the Oakland pinch hitter who struck out to end the fifth game?

16 On September 16, 1973, the Mets climbed within 2½ games of first place as they defeated the Cubs, 4–3, on a squeeze bunt by Jerry Grote in the bottom of the eighth inning. Which Met base runner scored on that play?

17 In the first game of the 1973 NLCS, Tom Seaver fanned thirteen Reds but lost 2–1 on two home runs. Who were the two Reds who homered in the eighth and ninth innings, respectively, giving Cincinnati the victory?

18 Which two outfielders who were in the starting lineup for the Montreal Expos in their first game in franchise history on April 8, 1969, at Shea Stadium later played for the Mets in 1973?

1986

1 The Mets used a total of nine starting pitchers in 1986. Five of them started twenty games or more. Who were the other four who didn't?

2 Which Met had the longest hitting streak (thirteen games) during the 1986 season?

3 Which Met started games at first base, shortstop, third base, and all three outfield positions in 1986?

4 Which pitcher led the 1986 world champion Mets with eighteen victories?

5 On June 10, this Met infielder came up as a pinch hitter for Wally Backman in the bottom of the eleventh inning and hit a game-ending grand slam to defeat the Phillies, 8–4. Can you name him?

6 On July 27 against the Atlanta Braves, three Mets hit consecutive home runs off Rick Mahler in a 5–1 Met win. Name the three Mets.

7 This Chicago Cub outfielder grounded out to Wally Backman for the last out of the game in the 1986 Eastern Division clincher on September 17. Later in his career, he played for the Mets in 1992 and 1993. Who is he?

8 In 1986, Doc Gooden became the first pitcher in major league history to have at least two hundred strikeouts in his first three seasons. He did this against the Montreal Expos in his last start of the regular season. The Expo batter who was strikeout victim 200 was the final batter Doc faced in this historic game, which took place on October 2, 1986, and later in his career, he played for the Mets in 1994. Who is this infielder?

9 The Mets lost game 1 of the 1986 National League Championship Series by a score of 1–0 to the Houston Astros. The Astro who homered against Doc Gooden in the third inning for the only run of the game was with the Mets in spring training of 1994 but did not make the team. Who is this ten-year veteran, who also played with the Baltimore Orioles?

10 Lenny Dykstra won game 3 of the 1986 NLCS with a two-run homer, giving the Mets a 6–5 win and a lead of two games to one in the series. Which Astro pitcher allowed Lenny's game-ending blast?

11 When Gary Carter drove in the winning run in the twelfth inning of game 5 of the 1986 NLCS, who was the Houston pitcher who gave up the winning hit?

12 What former Met pitcher had two complete game victories against the Mets in the 1986 NLCS?

13 Which two hurlers who pitched for the Red Sox in the 1986 World Series pitched for the Mets in 1985?

14 Lenny Dykstra led off game 3 of the 1986 World Series with a home run against which Boston pitcher?

15 During the 1986 postseason, two Mets from the twenty-four-man roster of players eligible to play did not appear in any game of either the National League Championship Series or the World Series. Name these two players.

16 What Met infielder hit a home run in the seventh inning of the final game of the 1986 World Series that put the Mets ahead to stay?

17 This San Francisco right-handed pitcher, who went 20–9 in 1986, was the only National League pitcher to defeat the Mets four times in 1986. Can you name this hurler who won 124 games with the Giants, Cubs, and Phillies and finished with a 22–7 lifetime record against the Mets?

18 On September 17, 1986, which was the night the Mets clinched the National League Eastern Division title, this rookie made his first major league start at first base, filling in for Keith Hernandez, who had a heavy cold. He collected three consecutive singles and drove in two runs, including the game winner. Who is this cousin of Lou Piniella?

19 Which former Cy Young Award winner was the starting pitcher for the Cubs when the Mets clinched the Eastern Division?

20 Who was the Mets on-deck hitter when Mookie Wilson's dribbler went by Red Sox first baseman Bill Buckner, giving the Mets a 6–5 win in game 6?

1988

1 On Opening Day (April 4), the Mets hit six homers in a game for the first time in their history. Darryl Strawberry and Kevin McReynolds each socked a pair. Who were the other two Mets who homered?

2 In an 11–3 Met victory over the Chicago Cubs on June 5, Dwight Gooden had a no-hitter for seven innings until this Cub catcher led off the eighth inning with a single. Can you name this backstop who also spent time with the Braves, Red Sox, Reds, and Giants?

3 During the 1988 All-Star Break, the Mets acquired two relief pitchers. One was signed as a free agent, who was formerly with the Expos. The other was acquired from Seattle for pitcher Gene Walter. Name both pitchers.

4 This Met outfielder set a major league record in 1988 when he stole twenty-one bases without being thrown out the entire season. Who is he?

5 Darryl Strawberry led all National Leaguers with thirty-nine homers in 1988. Which Astro finished second with thirty?

6 For the first time in club history, the Mets led the National League in home runs in 1988 with how many?

7 Which Met hurled a complete-game six-hitter in the Eastern Division clincher that the Mets won 3–1 on September 22, 1988?

8 The Phillie starter in the 1988 Eastern Division clincher threw a one-hit shutout against the Mets nearly one year before on September 28, 1987, with Mookie Wilson getting the only hit in a 3–0 Philadelphia win. Name this Phillie southpaw.

9 When the Mets clinched the 1988 Eastern Division crown against the Phillies, this former Tiger who was with Detroit from 1977 to 1986 struck out to end the game. Who is this backstop who went on to have a nineteen-year major league career?

10 In game 1 of the 1988 National League Championship Series at Los Angeles, the Mets were trailing 2–0 when they began the top of the ninth inning. New York rallied for three runs to win the game. Which two Mets belted RBI doubles to drive in three runs?

11 Which Dodger pitcher was ejected by umpire Harry Wendelstedt in game 3 of the NLCS for using a foreign substance on his glove?

12 In the fourth game of the 1988 NLCS, Kevin McReynolds was up in the bottom of the twelfth inning with two out and the bases loaded; he hit a looping fly that the Dodger center fielder caught to end the game. Name this LA center fielder who made the catch to protect a Dodger 5–4 lead.

13 With the Mets down three games to two, this Met hurler evened the series at three games each by tossing a 5–1 complete-game win, holding the Dodgers to five hits. Name him.

14 Which two Mets led the team with nine hits each in the 1988 NLCS?

15 Besides Orel Hershiser and Jesse Orosco, which two Dodger pitchers who appeared in the 1988 NLCS also pitched for the Mets at one time?

16 In 1988, the Mets moved to their new spring training facility in Port St. Lucie, Florida. In what Florida city did they train from 1962 to 1987?

1999

1 Who were the two Met pitchers who led the team with thirteen victories each in 1999?

2 On May 23, 1999, the Mets were trailing the Philadelphia Phillies, 4–0, going into the bottom of the ninth inning. Amazingly, they came up with five runs in the last of the ninth to win 5–4. Name the Phillie pitcher who went the distance and lost the game.

3 The Mets' longest hitting streak in 1999 was held by Mike Piazza. Mike hit in twenty-four straight games and tied the Met record for the longest hitting streak, which was first set in 1984 by whom?

4 On June 6, the Mets ended an eight-game losing streak by defeating the Yankees, 7–2. This started a run of forty victories in fifty-five games. Who was the Yankee losing pitcher?

5 The Mets set a major league record for fewest errors in a season in 1999. How many miscues did they commit?

6 In a seesaw battle in which the lead changed five times, the Mets and the Yankees played a classic game on July 10 at Shea Stadium. The Mets scored two runs in the bottom of the ninth to defeat the Yankees, 9–8. Which Met got the winning single off Yankee bull-pen ace Mariano Rivera?

7 In the same game, who were the two Met base runners who scored on that winning hit?

8 This pitcher, who was acquired from Oakland on July 23, led the Mets with two complete games. Name him.

9 Al Leiter hurled a 5–0 shutout over the Cincinnati Reds on October 4 in the play-off game that gave the Mets their wild card berth. Who was the Cincinnati Red losing pitcher in that game?

10 In the first game of the National League Division Series against Arizona on October 5, 1999, which player hit the first Met postseason grand slam in the team's history?

11 In the bottom of the eighth inning of the fourth game of the 1999 National League Division Series (NLDS), this Arizona right fielder made a costly error by not catching a fly ball hit by John Olerud. This error led to a game-tying sacrifice fly by Roger Cedeno. Who was the Diamondback right fielder who made this error?

12 What Arizona pitcher did Todd Pratt homer against to clinch the 1999 NLDS for the Mets?

13 Who was the Met winning pitcher in the game that Robin Ventura hit his "grand slam single" in the 1999 National League Championship Series?

14 Who was the Atlanta Brave pitcher who allowed Ventura's hit?

15 What Brave player scored the winning run for Atlanta in the eleventh inning of the final game of the 1999 NLCS?

16 Robin Ventura's eleventh-inning game-ending single with the bases loaded on October 1, 1999, against the Pirates gave the Mets a 3–2 win and helped them stay alive in their quest for a wild card berth. Which Brooklyn native scored the winning run?

17 On October 3, 1999, the Mets defeated the Pirates, 2–1, when they scored a run in the bottom of the ninth inning. This enabled them to face the Cincinnati Reds in a one-game play-off to determine the 1999 National League wild card winner. Mike Piazza was at bat when the Pirate pitcher threw a wild pitch that got by catcher Joe Oliver and scored Melvin Mora with the winning run. The Pirate moundsman who threw the pitch hurled for the Mets in 1998. Who is he?

2000

1 On March 30, 2000, the Mets played the Chicago Cubs in Japan. In the top of the eleventh inning, this pinch hitter batted for Dennis Cook and hit a grand slam off Cub reliever Danny Young, who was making his major league debut. Name the Met batter whose homer was the winning blow in a 5–1 Met victory.

2 In the Shea Stadium opener on April 3, Al Leiter was the winning pitcher in a 2–1 Met victory over San Diego. Which Met outfielder hit a home run off future Met pitcher Donnie Wall in the bottom of the eighth inning to put the Mets ahead to stay?

3 Who had the longest hitting streak (twenty games) for the Mets in 2000?

4 This Met infielder/outfielder hit his first career regular-season home run on April 20. It was a game-ending homer against Milwaukee's Curtis Leskanic and gave the Mets a 5–4 victory over the Brewers.

5 During the 2000 season, Mike Piazza had an RBI in fifteen consecutive games, breaking his own Met record of ten set in 1999. It was the second-longest consecutive RBI streak in major league history. The longest took place in 1922 by what Chicago Cub first baseman, who had an RBI in seventeen straight games?

6 In game 4 of the 2000 National League Division Series, which Giant and former Met smacked a double in the fifth inning off Bobby J. Jones for the only San Francisco hit in the final game of the series?

7 Which San Francisco relief pitcher gave up the home run that Benny Agbayani hit in the bottom of the thirteenth inning to beat the Giants, 3–2, in game 3 of the NLDS?

8 Which Giant flied out to center fielder Jay Payton to end the 2000 NLDS?

9 This former Met, who played five games for New York in 1998, made the last out of the 2000 National League Championship Series when he flied out to center fielder Timo Perez as the St. Louis Cardinals fell in five games. Name this backstop who in 1993 hit thirty homers for the Cubs.

10 Prior to the 2000 World Series, when was the last time that two teams from New York City clashed in the Fall Classic?

11 What former Met had four hits and drove in the winning run in the bottom of the twelfth inning in a 4–3 Yankee victory in game 1 of the 2000 World Series?

12 Benny Agbayani drove in the winning run in the bottom of the eighth inning of game 3 of the World Series, in a 4–2 Met win. Who did Benny drive in to give the Mets a 3–2 lead?

13 Who was the winning pitcher for the Mets in game 3 of the 2000 World Series?

14 The losing pitcher for the Yankees in game 3 entered the game with a postseason record of 8–0 and a 1.90 earned run average. Who is this pitcher?

15 Mike Piazza hit a home run in both Shea Stadium and Yankee Stadium during the 2000 World Series. Which two Yankee pitchers did he homer against?

16 Which member of the 2000 Mets is a direct descendant of two U.S. presidents, John Adams and John Quincy Adams?

17 The winning pitcher for the Yankees in the fifth and final game of the 2000 World Series signed with the Mets as a free agent after the 2002 season. Can you name this southpaw, who also hurled for the Braves from 1989 to 1995?

MISCELLANEOUS
METS TRIVIA

1962 ORIGINAL METS

1 What player led the Mets with thirty-four home runs and ninety-four runs batted in in 1962?

2 This Polo Grounds Met was second on the team with sixteen home runs in 1962 and had as his initials, M. E. T.

3 Who was the only pitcher with a winning record on the 1962 Mets?

4 In the first game of a doubleheader at the Polo Grounds on June 22, 1962, Al Jackson threw the club's first one-hitter. What Houston Colt 45 player who formerly played for the New York Giants collected a single in the first inning for Houston's only hit?

5 The Mets first home game at the Polo Grounds was on Friday April 13, 1962. They lost to the Pirates, 4–3. There were two men in the Met starting lineup who once played for the Brooklyn Dodgers. Can you name this pair?

6 In addition, there were two members of the Pirate starting lineup that day who played for the Mets at some point in their careers. Name them.

7 Who was the Met starting pitcher in the team's first home game at the Polo Grounds on April 13, 1962?

8 Al Jackson hurled all of the Mets' complete game shutouts in 1962. How many shutouts did he pitch?

9 Richie Ashburn collected his 2,500th hit on June 27, 1962, against Pittsburgh. The Pirate pitcher who gave up the milestone hit pitched for both the Mets and Yankees in 1966. Who is he?

10 On May 4, 1962, Don Zimmer broke an 0-for-34 slump with a double in the sixth inning off this Philadelphia Phillie pitcher, who hurled for the Mets for part of the 1966 season. Name him.

11 On May 12, the Mets swept a doubleheader from the Milwaukee Braves at the Polo Grounds by scores of 3–2 and 8–7. In each game, a Met player hit a home run in the bottom of the ninth inning to win the game. Name both Met batters.

12 What was the Mets' longest losing streak in 1962?

13 Which Met made the last out of Sandy Koufax's no-hitter on June 30, 1962?

14 On July 6, 1962, this Met hit the first grand slam in team history when he homered off the Cardinals' Bobby Shantz in a 10–3 romp over St. Louis. Who is this infielder/outfielder who was a Met from 1962 to 1964?

15 Which two members of the Met coaching staff died between the end of the 1962 season and the beginning of the 1963 season?

16 Who were the two members of the 1962 Mets who played in the Negro Leagues?

17 Which two members of the 1962 Mets had brothers who also played in the majors?

18 Of the twenty-two players who were selected in the expansion draft, held on October 10, 1961, only three of them played in the 1970s, and all finished their respective major league careers in 1974. Ironically, all three players were selected from the St. Louis Cardinal organization. Can you name this trio?

UNIFORM NUMBERS

1 When Willie Mays was acquired from the Giants in 1972, what Met relinquished number 24 and switched to number 5?

2 Who are the three Mets who wore number 16 between the time Doc Gooden left in 1994 and the start of the 2003 season?

3 What was the first uniform number officially retired by the Mets, and who wore it?

4 Who were the two Met players who wore number 14 besides Gil Hodges?

5 What is the highest uniform number worn by a Met player?

6 Which two Mets switched uniform numbers between the 1976 and 1977 seasons? (The numbers were 12 and 16.)

7 Which two players wore number 1 during the 1969 world championship season?

8 Tug McGraw, one of the most popular Mets in their history, wore number 45. What pitcher wore number 45 directly after McGraw was traded to the Phillies following the 1974 season?

9 Which Met who played the infield and outfield for New York from 1993 to 1998 wore number 42?

10 On September 1, 1996, Mookie Wilson was inducted into the New York Met Hall of Fame. Lance Johnson, who wore number 1 in 1996 and 1997, switched to a different number for that day only. What number?

11 During Roger Craig's eighteen-game losing streak in 1963, he switched his uniform number from 38 to what number?

12 Which two Mets wore number 24 after Willie Mays?

13 Who wore number 31 directly before Mike Piazza?

14 Who were the four Met pitchers who wore number 41 before Tom Seaver?

15 Edgardo Alfonzo wore number 13 from 1995 to 2002. This right-handed relief pitcher, who appeared in seven games in 1994 and lost his only decision, wore number 13 directly before Alfonzo. Who is he?

16 Ron Darling wore three different uniform numbers during his Met career. What were they?

17 From 1962 to 2002, a total of twenty-three Met players wore number 38, with twenty-two of them pitchers. This outfielder, who played in thirty-one games with the Mets in 1992, is the only position player thus far to wear this number. Who is he?

18 Who is the only Met *player* to wear number 54? (He wore it in 1996 and 1997.)

19 The two winners of the Sport Magazine Award for Most Valuable Player in the 1969 World Series and the 1986 World Series both wore the same uniform number for the Mets. Can you name both players and the number that they shared?

20 On April 6, 2003, Tony Clark made his Met debut and became the first Met player to wear number 00. Which outfielder in 1991 became the first Met to wear number 0?

TRADES

1 Jerry Grote was acquired by the Mets from the Houston organization on October 19, 1965, for a player to be named later. Name the pitcher who was sent to Houston on November 29, 1965, to complete the trade.

2 On November 18, 1994, the Mets traded outfielder Jeromy Burnitz and pitcher Joe Roa to the Cleveland Indians for pitchers Jerry Dipoto, Paul Byrd, a player to be named later (infielder Jesus Azuaje), and this pitcher, who in his first career complete game hurled a 6–0 shutout in the first ever regular-season meeting between the Mets and the Yankees at Yankee Stadium on June 16, 1997. Who is he?

3 On the trading deadline of July 31, 1989, the Mets traded five pitchers—Rick Aguilera, David West, Kevin Tapani, Tim Drummond, and Jack Savage—to acquire the 1988 American League Cy Young Award winner from the Minnesota Twins. Can you name this Long Island native?

4 In September 1970, the Mets acquired a pitcher from the Cleveland Indians for the stretch drive to help them in their quest to repeat as National League Eastern Division champs. (The Pirates won the division!) Who is this 1964 Cy Young Award winner?

5 Which two pitchers did the Mets send to St. Louis on June 15, 1983, to acquire Keith Hernandez?

6 Both Jerry Koosman and Jesse Orosco were on the mound for the final out of the 1969 and 1986 World Series, respectively. Ironically, they were traded for each other on December 8, 1978. What other pitcher (who never pitched in the major leagues) went from Minnesota to New York in that trade in addition to Orosco?

7 Between games of a doubleheader between the Mets and Phillies on August 2, 1979, the Mets purchased an outfielder from the Phillies. Can you name this eighteen-year veteran who played with nine teams in the big leagues?

8 In a four-team trade that involved the Mets, Braves, Pirates, and Rangers, the Mets traded Jon Matlack and John Milner and wound up with which three players?

9 On November 13, 1985, the Mets sent outfielders John Christensen and La Schelle Tarver and pitchers Calvin Schiraldi and Wes Gardner to the Boston Red Sox for a pitcher who led the 1986 World Champion Mets with eighteen victories. Name him.

10 What pitcher did the Mets send to Detroit in exchange for Howard Johnson?

11 Prior to the 2001 season, the last trade between the Mets and the Yankees took place on September 17, 1993, between two pitchers. The Mets received Kenny Greer. What pitcher who won 240 major league games did the Mets send to the Yankees?

12 Turk Wendell was acquired from the Chicago Cubs along with pitcher Mel Rojas and outfielder Brian McRae on August 8, 1997. What three Met players went to the Cubs in that deal?

13 On July 28, 2000, the Mets traded two former first-round draft picks, Paul Wilson (1994) and Jason Tyner (1998) to the Tampa Bay Devil Rays for which two players who helped the Mets to the National League pennant in 2000?

14 On the same day that the Mets traded Tom Seaver and Dave Kingman (June 15, 1997), the Mets acquired Joel Youngblood from the St. Louis Cardinals for what infielder?

15 On November 29, 1966, the Mets traded Ron Hunt and Jim Hickman to the Los Angeles Dodgers. In return, the Mets received infielder Derrell Griffith and this outfielder, who was born in Brooklyn, New York, and went to Boys High School in Brooklyn, where he was a teammate of NBA legend Lenny Wilkens on the basketball team. Name him.

16 Mike Piazza was acquired from the Florida Marlins on May 22, 1998, for three players. Name this trio.

17 The last active Brooklyn Dodger in the majors, who was also the last member of the original Houston Colt 45 team, was acquired by the Mets on December 1, 1970, from the Atlanta Braves for pitcher Ron Herbel. Who is this alumnus of Lafayette High School in Brooklyn, who also had a brother who played in the big leagues from 1957 to 1963?

18 This Met third baseman, who had four hits in his Met debut, was acquired from the Philadelphia Phillies along with minor league infielder José Moreno for pitcher Nino Espinosa on March 27, 1979. Who is he?

ROOKIES

1 Three days after he made his major league debut, this rookie drove in two runners with a double in the bottom of the ninth, which gave the Mets a 5–4 victory over the Milwaukee Braves on April 19, 1963. This was the Mets' first victory after eight consecutive losses to start the season. Who is this hard-nosed rookie?

2 This rookie pitcher made his major league debut a successful one when he defeated Jim Maloney and the Cincinnati Reds with a 5–0 complete-game shutout on June 10, 1966. Name him.

3 On June 13, 2001, the Mets came back from a six-run deficit to beat the Baltimore Orioles, 7–6, in ten innings at Camden Yards. This rookie's RBI single scored Mike Piazza in the top half of the tenth inning for the winning run. Who is he?

4 On September 13, 1996, this rookie pitcher in a game against Atlanta struck out Terry Pendleton (who reached base on a passed ball), Chipper Jones, Ryan Klesko, and Mike Mordecai in the ninth inning to become the first Met pitcher to strike out four batters in one inning. Can you name him?

5 This 1979 first-round draft pick made his major league debut on April 12, 1981, at Wrigley Field. He was the starting pitcher and left after only two innings because of elbow stiffness in forty-six-degree weather. Can you name this former UCLA Bruin?

6 In his fourth game since joining the Mets, this rookie on June 21, 1977, hit a three-run homer in the bottom of the eleventh inning off Atlanta's Don Collins to give the Mets a 5–2 victory. Who is he?

7 This rookie, who was born in England and was the Mets first selection in the June 1965 draft, made his major league debut on September 19, 1967, and beat the Dodgers and Bill Singer, 6–3. Can you name him?

8 This rookie hit for the cycle on July 3, 1996, in only his twenty-second major league game, which was the third-fastest cycle in major league history. Name this outfielder.

9 This rookie made his major league debut on September 8, 1993, and went hitless in three trips to the plate, with three strikeouts in the game that Darryl Kile threw a no-hitter against the Mets. Name him.

10 This rookie hit in twenty-three consecutive games in 1975, a record for Met rookies that still stands. Who is he?

11 This rookie, who missed two years in the minor leagues because of military service (including a stint in Vietnam), made his major league debut on July 14, 1972, against the San Diego Padres. In his third major league at bat, he hit a home run off San Diego's Steve Arlin, which gave the Mets a 3–2 victory over the Padres. Who is this outfielder?

12 On August 4, 1975, a Met pitcher held the Montreal Expos hitless for 7⅓ innings until Jim Lyttle's pinch single ended the no-hit bid. Name this pitcher who only pitched in the major leagues for one season.

13 This "hard luck" rookie from Lost Nation, Iowa, had very little run support in his first major league season. The Mets were shut out in his first four starts and in five of his seven losses in 1968. Name this right-handed pitcher whose son pitched the major leagues in the 1990s.

14 On August 14, 1962, Al Jackson became the first Met starting pitcher to go fifteen innings but lost to the Phillies by a score of 3–1. This Met rookie who made his major league debut on September 1, 1965, was the only other Met to pitch fifteen innings, when he did it just about a month later on October 2, also against the Phillies. Who is he?

15 This rookie pitched a one-hitter in his rookie season (1991) against the Montreal Expos. Can you name this right-hander who also toiled for the Red Sox twice, along with the Reds, Astros, and Pirates?

16 Ron Swoboda set a Met record for home runs by a rookie with nineteen in 1965. Which original Met had the previous record of thirteen in 1962?

17 This pitcher made his major league debut on September 2, 1965, when he defeated the Cardinals, 6–3. Ten days later, he beat Milwaukee, 1–0, in ten innings and set a then–Mets club record with thirteen strike-outs. Can you name this right-hander who also pitched for the Padres, Cubs, Phillies, Angels, and Brewers?

18 Which Met rookie appeared as a pinch runner for Matt Franco and scored from third base on a balk by Yankee pitcher David Cone in the eighth inning that tied up the game, 2–2, on June 18, 1997?

19 This man, who played ten years in the majors, made his big league debut on April 14, 1964. He struck out for the final out in Jim Bunning's perfect game on June 21, 1964. Who is this backstop who also played for the Cubs, Giants, and Angels?

20 This rookie, whose only big league season was 1963, was the last major league batter in the Polo Grounds. As a pinch hitter, he grounded into a double play in the ninth inning in a 5–1 loss to the Phillies. Can you name this infielder who played ball at James Madison High School in Brooklyn and later played at St. John's University?

21 In 1972, this Met rookie was the first winner of the John J. Murphy Award, which is given to the top Met rookie in spring training. He also led the Mets in home runs that year with seventeen. Who is he?

NICKNAMES

1 This 1962 Met had the nickname of "Whitey." Who was he?

2 This 1963 Met infielder was known as "Possum." He was acquired from the Dodgers after the 1962 season. Can you name him?

3 He played 247 games at third base for the Mets and was known as "The Glider." Who is this member of the 1969 world championship team?

4 Can you name this player who was very instrumental in the 1969 world championship year and had the nickname "Clink"?

5 Who was known as "Choo Choo"?

6 Which utility infielder, who played for the Mets in the mid- to late 1960s, was known as "Casey" because of his initials?

7 Can you name this pitcher who toiled for the Mets from 1964 to 1967 and was known as "Fat Jack"?

8 This pitcher, who appeared in eighty-four games for the Mets in 1979 and 1980, was called "The Flushing Flash." Can you name him?

9 This wiry left-handed relief pitcher was known as "The Blade."

10 Which pitcher was known as "Hairbreath Harry"?

11 This man who played with the Cardinals, Mets, Yankees, Cubs, and White Sox is known as "One Dog." Who is he?

12 Which early-day Met was known as "Hot Rod"?

13 This pitcher who was with the Mets from 1968 to 1973 is "The Pride of Lost Nation, Iowa."

14 What Polo Ground Met who played eighteen years in the majors, including eleven years in a Brooklyn Dodger uniform, was "The Silver Fox"?

15 Can you name this 1966 Met who was known as "Dr. Strangeglove"?

16 What outfielder, who was a member of the 1973 National League pennant–winning team was "The Stork"?

17 Besides Rusty Staub, the Mets had another player nicknamed "Rusty." In 1982, he appeared in twelve games as a pinch hitter/ outfielder. Can you name him?

18 This Met twenty-game winner was nicknamed "Sweet Music." Can you name him?

19 Even though he never played for the Mets, can you identify this longtime third base coach who was known as "The Walking Man"?

20 What pitcher who had a 5–35 record for the Mets in three seasons was "A.Y."?

21 These three Met pitchers who made their major league debuts in 1995 and 1996, respectively, were collectively known as "Generation K." Can you name this trio?

22 This three-year Met from 1965 to 1967, who was primarily a second baseman, was known as "Iron Hands."

23 This Met coach and interim manager was known as "The Capital Punisher." Who is he?

24 This 1962 Met was nicknamed "Popeye." Who is he?

ALL-STARS

1 Who was the first Met to play in an All-Star Game?

2 In 1964, Ron Hunt was voted as the starting second baseman for the National League. He became the first Met ever to start an All-Star Game. Hunt had one hit in three trips to the plate. He singled against an American League pitcher who would pitch three games for the Mets in 1970. Can you name this pitcher?

3 The 1964 All-Star Game was the only time that it was held at Shea Stadium. What Philadelphia Phillie outfielder hit a home run in the bottom of the ninth inning to win the game for the National League, 7–4?

4 Tom Seaver became the first Met to pitch in an All-Star Game when he appeared in the fifteenth inning in 1967. What future Hall of Famer was the winning pitcher for the National League?

5 In his first All-Star appearance in 1968, Jerry Koosman struck out this future Hall of Famer for the final out to preserve a 1–0 National League victory.

6 Which Met collected two hits and scored two runs in the 1969 All-Star Game as the National League won, 9–3?

7 Dwight Gooden was the youngest player ever selected to the All-Star Game when he was chosen in 1984 at the age of nineteen. In the first inning he worked, he struck out the side. Name the three American League batters he fanned.

8 Besides Doc Gooden, the only other Met pitcher to start an All-Star Game is Tom Seaver. What year did Tom make his only National League start as a Met?

9 The year 1973 marked the twenty-fourth and final time that Willie Mays appeared in an All-Star Game. In his last All-Star appearance, Willie struck out against which Yankee pitcher?

10 Jon Matlack was the winning pitcher for the National League in the 1975 All-Star Game as the National League won, 6–3. Matlack was named Co–Most Valuable Player of the game. With which Chicago Cub player did Jon share the MVP award?

11 Which Met pitcher was named to the 1978 National League All-Star Team but was replaced because of an injury?

12 Lee Mazzilli was the first member of the New York Mets to belt a home run in an All-Star Game when he homered in the 1979 game at the Kingdome in Seattle. Which Texas Ranger hurler gave up Lee's homer?

13 In that same game, Mazzilli drove in the winning run in the top of the ninth inning with a bases-loaded walk, giving the National League a 7–6 win. Which Yankee pitcher allowed the walk?

14 Which Yankee first baseman did Sid Fernandez strike out in his first All-Star appearance in the 1986 game in Houston?

15 Who were the other four Met players besides Fernandez who were on the 1986 NL All-Star Team?

16 In the 1988 All-Star Game, Dwight Gooden was the National League starting and losing pitcher. The opposing American League starter was the winning pitcher and was Doc's teammate from 1989 to 1991. Who is this three-time All-Star?

17 What year did Jerry Grote appear for the National League as the starting catcher?

RECORD HOLDERS

1 Tom Seaver was elected to the Baseball Hall of Fame in 1992 with 98.84 percent, the highest percentage of votes ever cast for a Hall of Famer. Who had the previous high of 98.23 percent, which was set in 1936?

2 The Met record holder for career pinch home runs is eight and is held by the son of a former American League catcher who played from 1959 to 1966. Can you name this Met?

3 The Met record going into the 2003 season for most doubles in one game by a batter is three. It has been accomplished eighteen times. The first time was on May 14, 1964, by this first baseman/outfielder who made his Met debut in 1963. Who is he?

4 In 1965, Ron Swoboda had ten home runs in his first ninety at bats. That mark was broken in 1999 when it took this player only seventy-three at bats to reach ten home runs. Name this outfielder.

5 The Met record for most starting assignments by a pitcher in one season is thirty-six. It is held by two pitchers. Tom Seaver started thirty-six games for the Mets in 1970, 1973, and 1975. It was first accomplished by a Met hurler in 1965. Name this man who was the Mets' winning pitcher when they beat Juan Marichal (19−0) and Larry Jackson (18−0) for the first time.

6 Who has the Met record for most outfield assists in one season with nineteen?

7 This Met infielder set a National League record and tied a major league record by grounding into four double plays in one game on July 21, 1975. Name him.

8 This Met set a team record and tied a National League record by reaching base fifteen consecutive times in 1998. Who is he?

9 The Met record for a player homering in consecutive games is four. Who are the seven Mets who accomplished this feat?

10 This outfielder set a team record with five RBIs in one inning against the Florida Marlins on May 26, 1988. Who is he?

11 Roger Craig holds the Met record for most home runs allowed in one season. How many gopher balls did Roger give up?

12 On April 22, 1970, Tom Seaver fanned nineteen batters, including the last ten in a row, which set a major league record. What team did he face when he set this record?

13 The tenth consecutive strikeout victim also played for the Los Angeles Dodgers and the Cincinnati Reds in a career that ended in 1971. Who is this Brooklyn-born outfielder who graduated from Lafayette High School, which also produced Hall of Fame pitcher Sandy Koufax and Mets owner Fred Wilpon?

14 Who holds the Met record for most runs batted in for one game?

15 Going into the 2003 season, four players in Met history have struck out five times in one game. Who are they?

16 On May 1, 1980, this Brooklyn-born left-handed pitcher tied a major league record by striking out the first six batters to face him in a starting assignment against the Phillies. Who is this alumnus of Lafayette High School in Brooklyn?

17 On October 6, 1991, David Cone struck out nineteen Phillies to tie Tom Seaver's Met record of most strikeouts in a game. Cone allowed three hits as the Mets blanked the Phillies, 7–0. Which Phillie infielder was the nineteenth victim?

TWO-TERM METS

1 This pitcher was acquired from Detroit on May 30, 1964. Then he was traded to Milwaukee for Dennis Ribant on August 8. He was reacquired by the Mets during spring training in 1965 and traded to the White Sox for catcher Jimmie Schaffer on July 8. Name this first two-term Met.

2 What two-term Met who played for the Mets in 1980 and 1987 was the first overall selection in the 1974 free agent draft by the Padres?

3 This two-term Met had the only hit (a home run in the fifth inning) allowed by Curt Schilling in a game that the Mets lost to the Phillies, 2–1, at Veterans Stadium on September 9, 1992. He also smacked home runs from both sides of the plate four times as a Met. Who is this graduate of Lehman High School in the Bronx?

4 He was a first-round draft pick of the New York Mets in 1978 and was a teammate of Bob Horner at Arizona State University. Who is he?

5 Which two-term Met infielder was called "Crazy Horse"?

6 This two-term Met appeared against the Mets in the 1999 National League Division Series with Arizona. Name him.

7 This two-term Met batted .417 in the 1980 World Series for the Kansas City Royals. Can you name him?

8 Besides Tom Seaver, who is the other two-term Met who played for the Mets in the 1960s, 1970s, and 1980s?

9 This man pitched for New York in 1981 and 1982. He returned to the Met organization in 1984 after starting the season for the Richmond team in the International League. His best season as a Met was 1987 when he had an 11–1 record. Who is he?

10 This pitcher began the 1998 season with the Mets but was traded to the Dodgers along with pitcher Dave Mlicki on June 5 for pitchers Hideo Nomo and Brad Clontz. He was then reacquired from the Dodgers on July 10 for pitcher Brian Bohanon. He thus became the first player to play for the Mets on two separate occasions in the same season. Who is this right-handed relief specialist?

11 This two-term Met hit for the cycle against the Cardinals on August 1, 1989, and led the Mets in outfield assists from 1987 to 1991. Who is he?

12 This two-term Met pitched for the St. Louis Cardinals in the 1964 World Series. Name him.

13 Which twenty-three-year major league veteran played for the Mets twice and the Expos twice?

14 Who is the only two-term Met to play for them in the 1970s, 1980s, and 1990s?

15 This relief pitcher played for the Mets twice and the Boston Red Sox twice in the 1990s. Who is he?

16 Which two-term Met stole home against the Yankees at Yankee Stadium on June 29, 2002?

17 There have been two two-term Mets whose second term with the Mets was at least ten years after leaving the Mets the first time. Can you name these two pitchers?

HALL OF FAME OPPONENTS

1 Four members of the Hall of Fame hit at least forty-five home runs against the Mets. Can you name this quartet?

2 This Hall of Fame pitcher went ten innings in the famous twenty-three-inning game of May 31, 1964, and got credit for the victory. Who is he?

3 Which Hall of Fame pitcher drove in the only run of the game by hitting a home run off Warren Spahn in a 1–0 Met defeat on May 5, 1965?

4 Which Hall of Famer hit the first home run in Shea Stadium on April 17, 1964?

5 This Hall of Famer's single on April 11, 1962, drove in the first run scored against the Mets in their history. Name him.

6 This Hall of Famer hit the first home run ever against the Mets when he homered against Al Jackson on April 14, 1962. Who is he?

7 Which Hall of Fame pitcher won the most games against the Mets (thirty) and lost the most games against the Mets (thirty-six) than any other pitcher from 1962 to 2002?

8 This Hall of Famer on May 31, 1964, stole home against the Mets in the first game of a doubleheader and lined into a triple play in the "nightcap" that lasted twenty-three innings. Who is he?

9 This Hall of Famer hit three home runs against the Mets twice in his career: September 22, 1963, and September 17, 1966. Can you name him?

10 This Hall of Famer slugged his three hundredth career homer against the Mets on July 26, 1978, at Shea. Who is he?

11 Which Cub Hall of Famer broke up Gary Gentry's bid for a no-hitter with two outs in the eighth inning on May 13, 1970?

12 Gentry had another no-hit bid broken up by a future Hall of Famer on April 18, 1971, when this Pirate tripled in the sixth inning. Can you name him?

13 This Hall of Famer delivered a sixth-inning RBI single for the only run of the game as Tom Seaver lost 1–0 at Wrigley Field on July 14, 1969. Who is he?

14 Which pitcher hit a grand slam against the Mets on July 26, 1973?

15 Name the pitcher who had a 26–8 record against the Mets and was 19–0 before losing for the first time on July 4, 1967.

16 This pitcher gave up a home run to Tommie Agee to lead off game 3 of the 1969 World Series. Name him.

17 This man hit a game-ending home run for the Dodgers against the Mets on July 18, 1972. On May 25, 1983, while as manager of the Giants, he reprimanded pitcher Jim Barr on the mound at Shea Stadium when he took Barr out of the game in the seventh inning and Barr refused to wait for the new pitcher (Greg Minton). Who is this Hall of Famer who was inducted in 1982?

18 This pitcher had a 17–2 record against the Mets from 1962 to 1966. Name him?

19 Which three members of the 1973 Oakland A's are in the Hall of Fame and played against the Mets in the 1973 World Series?

RALPH KINER

1 These two longtime "Voices of the Pittsburgh Pirates" broadcast many of Kiner's home run heroics. Can you name this pair?

2 What was the name of Ralph's postgame TV show that aired on WOR-TV Channel 9 in New York for many years?

3 How many home runs did Ralph hit in his major league career?

4 Ralph homered every 14.11 times at bat, which was the second best in major league history when he retired after the 1955 season. Which slugger is first all-time with a home run ratio of 11.76?

5 Kiner has the most home runs for any major leaguer born in the state of New Mexico. This American League slugging shortstop who played from 1941 to 1955 is second with 247 round-trippers. Who is this player, who was nicknamed "Junior"?

6 In his ten-year career, Kiner batted over .300 three times. What was his highest batting average for one season?

7 Kiner either led or tied for the National League lead in home runs for seven consecutive years (1946–1952). Which slugging Hall of Fame first baseman (then with the New York Giants) shared the NL home run crown with Ralph in 1947 and 1948?

8 When Kiner led the National League in home runs with twenty-three in 1946, it marked the first time since 1902 that a Pirate led the NL in home runs. Can you name the Pirate third baseman who led the league with six home runs in 1902?

9 Kiner homered against 147 different pitchers during his career. The pitcher who allowed the most home runs to Kiner, with twelve, hurled for the New York Giants from 1947 to 1954 and won 120 games during that span. Can you name this right-handed pitcher who won at least twenty games for the Giants twice during his career, including his rookie season?

10 Prior to the 1947 season, the Pirates acquired a future Hall of Famer who led the American League in home runs (44) and runs batted in (127) in 1946. Kiner and this man combined for seventy-six homers in 1947. Who is this baseball great who became Ralph's friend and mentor?

11 In only his third major league season, Kiner became the Pirate career home run king. Which Pittsburgh Hall of Fame outfielder who played with the Pirates from 1926 to 1940 held the old team record of 109 home runs?

12 Ralph hit for the cycle against what team on June 25, 1950?

13 What future Hall of Fame outfielder fractured his elbow while making a catch off the bat of Kiner in the 1950 All-Star Game?

14 On May 6, 1951, Kiner appeared in a game in which the Pirate pitcher threw a no-hitter as Pittsburgh defeated the Boston Braves by a score of 3–0. It was the only no-hitter that Kiner ever participated in. The Pirate southpaw who pitched this gem was subsequently traded to the Cardinals later that season. Can you name this hurler who went 14–12 in 1951?

15 Kiner became the twelfth player in major league history to hit three hundred homers when he homered against the New York Giants at Forbes Field on May 25, 1953. This right-handed hurler who relinquished the historic home run had a 6–4 record with the Giants in 1953 in forty-eight games. Who is this Newburgh, New York, native?

16 Ralph was traded from Pittsburgh on June 4, 1953, to the Chicago Cubs with three other players in exchange for six players and $150,000. Can you name the trio of players who went with Kiner to the Windy City?

17 Can you name the Hall of Fame executive who was the Pirate general manager at the time Kiner was traded to the Cubs?

18 Which three members of the 1962 Mets were once Pittsburgh Pirate teammates of Kiner?

19 Kiner had 301 homers while in a Pittsburgh uniform and held the Pirate record for lifetime home runs until this future Hall of Famer passed him in 1973. Who is this first baseman/outfielder who had 475 home runs for the Buccos?

20 Who were the regular center fielder and right fielder for the Cubs when Ralph joined them in 1953?

21 Kiner hit eighteen home runs in his last major league season (1955). Which American League team did he play for during that season?

22 After his playing days were completed, Ralph became the general manager for which Pacific Coast League club from 1956 to 1960?

23 In 1961, Ralph shared the radio booth with two Ford Frick Award recipients: Bob Elson and Milo Hamilton. Can you name the American League team that Kiner was employed with that season?

24 What year was Kiner elected to the Baseball Hall of Fame?

25 Accompanying Ralph to the Hall of Fame that same year was a second baseman who played in the National League for fifteen seasons, primarily with the Cubs. This "keystoner" also played with Brooklyn and the Boston Braves before becoming a player-manager with the Pirates in 1947, Ralph's second year in the majors. Can you name him?

26 In September 1987, Kiner had his uniform number officially retired by the Pirates. What number did he wear as a Pirate?

LINDSEY NELSON

1 What article of clothing did Lindsey wear that made him unique?

2 At the 1940 Rose Bowl, Lindsey was a spotter for which legendary sports reporter from NBC Radio?

3 Lindsey graduated from college in 1941 and returned to his alma mater during his semiretirement and taught sports broadcasting. Can you name the Southeastern Conference school that he attended?

4 In the summer of 1945, Lindsey was in the army and stationed in Austria. He did some announcing for an army baseball team who had as its manager a future National League batting champion (1947). This man later managed the Cardinals, Pirates, and Astros. Can you name this outfielder?

5 Starting in 1951, Lindsey worked for a network that broadcast re-creations of major league games in non–major league cities. Name this network.

6 The founder of this network was known as "The Old Scotchman." Can you name this man that Lindsey worked for?

7 While Nelson was on the NBC television network he called games with which future baseball Hall of Famer who at one time or another wore the uniform of the Brooklyn Dodgers, New York Giants, and the New York Yankees?

8 In the mid- to late 1950s, Lindsey broadcast NCAA football for NBC television with a college football legend nicknamed "The Galloping Ghost." Who is this gridiron great?

9 Lindsey announced games for a major independent college football team for thirteen years. Name this midwestern school.

10 Who is the 1956 Heisman Trophy winner who was Lindsey's analyst for some of these games?

11 In 1965, Lindsey broadcast a Met road game from a gondola 208 feet in the air that was situated behind second base. In what stadium (which is no longer used for baseball) did this take place?

12 What was the name of the book that Lindsey cowrote with Al Hirshberg in 1966 that described his first four seasons as a Met broadcaster?

13 Lindsey did preseason games for the Chicago Bears in 1966. During that period, he hired a spotter who later in life became a major sports announcer for CBS. Can you name him?

14 On October 31, 1966, CBS televised an "experimental" Monday night football game between the Chicago Bears and St. Louis Cardinals. Lindsey did the play-by-play. His partner in the booth that night eventually became a fixture on ABC's *Monday Night Football* a few years later. Who is this former New York Giant?

15 What were the call letters of the New Jersey AM radio station that Lindsey, Ralph Kiner, and Bob Murphy were on during the 1969 world championship season?

16 Lindsey left the Mets after the 1978 season. Which National League team did he announce for three years from 1979 to 1981?

17 Who replaced Lindsey in 1979 as the third member of the New York Met broadcast team?

18 For over twenty years, Lindsey broadcast this major college football game on New Year's Day. Can you name this bowl game, which is played in Texas?

19 Lindsey did the radio broadcasts of *Monday Night Football* from 1974 to 1977. On what broadcast system, which was formed in 1934, did he call these games?

20 In 1979, Lindsey was inducted into the National Sportscasters and Sportswriters Hall of Fame. Which United States Vietnam War general and a close personal friend introduced Lindsey at this event?

21 Although he had retired from broadcasting, Lindsey made a guest appearance in the New York Yankee television booth on August 4, 1985, to broadcast the ninth inning of a game between the Yankees and the Chicago White Sox. What was the significance of this game?

22 What year was Lindsey inducted into the Broadcasters' Wing of the Baseball Hall of Fame in Cooperstown, New York?

BOB MURPHY

1 Bob is the younger brother of the late Jack Murphy, a newspaper columnist who was very instrumental in bringing major league baseball to the city of San Diego. Can you name the San Diego newspaper that employed Jack Murphy?

2 During World War II, in which branch of the military did Bob serve while stationed in the South Pacific?

3 What college that is presently in the Western Athletic Conference did Murphy attend, where he was a petroleum engineering major?

4 Bob called college football games for this Big Twelve school that was coached by Bud Wilkinson. Can you name it?

5 Bob's first major league broadcasting assignment started in 1954 and lasted for six seasons. Which American League team did "Murph" broadcast for through 1959 that had future Mets Pumpsie Green, Herb Moford, and Jimmy Piersall?

6 During this assignment, Bob was teamed up with this Hall of Fame broadcaster who won the Ford C. Frick Award in 1984. Can you name this man who also did Yankee games on radio with Mel Allen in 1949 and 1950 and later did football and baseball for NBC television, including the Jets Super Bowl and the Mets World Series victories in 1969?

7 In 1960 and 1961, Murphy did games for another American League team, where he saw future Mets Jack Fisher, Joe Ginsberg, Marv Throneberry, and Gene Woodling. He worked with Herb Carneal, who won the Frick Award in 1996. Name this team, which won their first World Series in 1966.

8 Murphy was the first radio announcer that Met fans heard on Opening Night in St. Louis on April 11, 1962. What AM radio station, which was also known for playing rock and roll oldies, broadcast the Met games during the Polo Grounds years of 1962 and 1963?

9 In 1962, Bob broadcast football games for the New York Titans of the American Football League. Bob also did the games in 1963 when the Titans became the New York Jets. Which baseball Hall of Famer, who played in the Negro Leagues as well as the New York Giants and the Chicago Cubs, served as the analyst for the Jets in 1963?

10 Who replaced Murphy as New York Jet announcer in 1964 and stayed with the Jets through the 1972 season?

11 During the 1980s, Murphy called two postseason college bowl games while working for NBC Radio. Can you name these two Florida-based bowl games?

12 In 1982, the Mets made a major change, and Murphy did Met games on radio only, while Kiner did games exclusively on television. Can you name Murphy's radio colleague from 1982 to 1984?

13 Can you name this attorney who was Murphy's broadcast partner and sidekick in the Met radio booth from 1985 to 1988?

14 Bob broadcast his first World Series in 1986. What AM station were the Mets on during that championship season?

15 Murphy's current radio partner began his Met career in 1989. Who is this Ivy League–educated Queens native who also does college basketball play-by-play for St. Johns University?

16 Which WFAN radio personality fills in for Bob occasionally during the season as Murphy now works a reduced schedule?

17 What year did Murphy enter the Baseball Hall of Fame by winning the Frick Award in ceremonies that were held in Cooperstown, New York?

18 At the conclusion of every Met victory, what phrase does Murphy say before going into a commercial break?

ANSWER KEY

Mets Trivia: The Players

Tommie Agee

1. Cleon Jones
2. Grambling
3. 1966
4. Al Weis
5. Bob Gibson
6. Larry Jackson
7. Don Bosch scored the winning run, and Gerry Arrigo took the loss.
8. Larry Jaster
9. Willie Davis
10. 26 home runs
11. St. Louis Cardinals
12. Jim Brewer
13. 107 runs, breaking his team record of 97, set in 1969
14. George Stone
15. Mel McGaha

Edgardo Alfonzo

1. Jeff Fassero
2. Bobby Bonilla, who played in 46 games
3. Matt Grott
4. Bud Harrelson against Pittsburgh on August 17, 1967; Don Hahn against Philadelphia on September 5, 1971; and Timo Perez on September 24, 2000, also against Philadelphia
5. 20 games
6. Donovan Osborne
7. Kevin Tapani
8. Manny Aybar
9. Jeff Kent
10. Lance Johnson in 1996

11. 191 in 1999
12. Most runs scored (6) and most total bases (16)
13. Four: 1997 (.315), 1999 (.304), 2000 (.324), and 2002 (.308)
14. Ricky Bottalico
15. Lenny Randle
16. Dave Concepcion of the Cincinnati Reds
17. Fernando Valenzuela

Wally Backman

1. 1977
2. Dave Goltz
3. Rick Camp
4. Enrique Romo
5. Bob Bailor (SS) and Dave Kingman (1B)
6. Mike Fitzgerald
7. Keith Hernandez
8. 32 bases
9. 1985
10. Hubie Brooks
11. Tim Burke
12. 1985
13. Darryl Strawberry at second base and Gary Carter on third base
14. David Cone
15. The Seattle Mariners

Gary Carter

1. "Kid"
2. Steve Carlton
3. Charlie Lea
4. Ken Forsch and Ron Davis
5. Infielder Hubie Brooks, outfielder Herm Winningham, pitcher Floyd Youmans, and catcher Mike Fitzgerald
6. Neil Allen
7. Mario Soto
8. Ray Knight
9. San Diego Padres
10. Mike LaValliere
11. Rusty Staub
12. Wally Backman
13. Mark Bomback

14. Mike Torrez

15. Al Nipper

16. Paul Assnemacher

17. Al Lopez

18. Johnny Bench, Yogi Berra, and Carlton Fisk

19. Eddie Murray

20. .294

21. Randy Sterling

22. Jon Matlack

23. Whitey Ford was the starting pitcher and Yogi Berra was the starting catcher in a game at Yankee Stadium.

24. Bob Walk

25. Barry Foote

26. Lance Parrish

David Cone

1. Jerry Reuss

2. Atlee Hammaker

3. Tom Seaver in 1969 and Bobby Jones in 1997

4. Preacher Roe

5. Joe Magrane with a 2.18 ERA

6. John Franco

7. Herm Winningham and Randy Myers

8. Benny Distefano

9. Bobby Ojeda, Frank Tanana, and Mike Torrez

10. 1990 with 233 and 1991 with 241

11. John Olerud

12. Bob Shawkey

13. Infielder Jeff Kent and outfielder Ryan Thompson

14. Kansas City Royals

15. Shortstop Orlando Cabrera popped out to third baseman Scott Brosius.

16. Mike Piazza, who popped out to second baseman Luis Sojo

17. Five: 1992 with Toronto and 1996, 1998, 1999, 2000 with the Yankees

18. The Oakland A's

19. Number 44 (1987–1991) and number 17 (1991–1992)

20. Tomo Ohka

Ron Darling

1. Yale University

2. Frank Viola

3. Lee Mazzilli

4. Lee Tunnell

5. Los Angeles Dodgers

6. 1985

7. Tom Gorman

8. John Tudor

9. 2.81

10. Greg Gross

11. Vince Coleman

12. 17 wins in 1988

13. Floyd Youmans (Philadelphia) and Norm Charlton (Cincinnati)

14. 1989

15. 99 wins

16. Mets: Terry Blocker; Padres: Kevin McReynolds; White Sox: Darryl Boston

Lenny Dykstra

1. "Nails"

2. Mario Soto

3. 8, which ties him with Tommie Agee

4. 1986 with 7 triples and 31 stolen bases

5. .295 in 1986

6. Bob Welch

7. Bob Sebra

8. Felix Millan (1975) and Joel Youngblood (1979)

9. Dennis Martinez

10. Mike Bielecki

11. David Cone

12. Chuck Klein

13. Tony Gwynn

14. 4 home runs

15. Dave Stewart

16. Mickey Morandini

Sid Fernandez

1. Infielder Bob Bailor and pitcher Carlos Diaz

2. Benny Agbayani

3. Mike Scott

4. Von Hayes

5. 1986 with 200

6. 1986

7. 16 in 1986
8. Houston Astros
9. Ron Darling
10. Terry Mulholland
11. 1989 (2.83) and 1992 (2.73)
12. 1985 (.181), 1988 (.191), and 1990 (.200)
13. Dan Quisenberry
14. 9 shutouts
15. Lonnie Smith
16. Jim Rice, Dwight Evans, Rich Gedman, and Spike Owen

John Franco

1. Los Angeles Dodgers
2. Lafayette High School
3. Larry Bearnarth
4. Bruce Berenyi
5. 11 games
6. 6 in 1992
7. Dave Righetti
8. Orel Hershiser
9. Ron Taylor
10. 1988 (39), 1990 (33), and 1994 (30)
11. 274 saves
12. Trevor Hoffman
13. Lee Smith
14. Randy Myers
15. 1992 (1.64) and 1996 (1.83)
16. Vern Rapp
17. Anthony Young

Dwight Gooden

1. Shawon Dunston
2. Rich Puig
3. Floyd Youmans
4. Dickie Thon
5. Doug Frobel
6. Rick Rhoden
7. 10 games
8. Jim Gott
9. Bob Gibson

10. Bob Feller, who was 20 years, 10 months, and 5 days in 1939
11. Sandy Koufax
12. John Tudor
13. Barry Bonds
14. Mike Dunne
15. Tim Teufel
16. David Nied
17. Paul Sorrento, who popped out to shortstop Derek Jeter
18. Bobby Ojeda (1987) and David Cone (1992)
19. The Tampa Bay Devil Rays and the Houston Astros
20. Gary Sheffield
21. 1,875 strikeouts
22. 157 wins

Jerry Grote
1. Al Jackson
2. Rusty Staub
3. Ken Johnson
4. Lew Burdette
5. 1,176 games
6. Harry Craft
7. Jerry Arrigo
8. Chris Cannizzaro
9. Dave Marshall and Joe Foy
10. 8
11. Wayne Granger
12. Joe Pepitone
13. Steve Arlin
14. Mike Phillips
15. The Kansas City Royals
16. Bobby Wine
17. Dick Selma and Chris Short

Bud Harrelson
1. Derrel
2. June 6, 1944 (D-Day)
3. Eddie Bressoud (94 games) and Roy McMillan (71 games)
4. Jerry Buchek
5. Juan Pizarro
6. Grant Jackson

7. 95 walks

8. Tim Harkness on September 9, 1963

9. 1971

10. Jack Billingham

11. Philadelphia Phillies (for minor league infielder Fred Andrews)

12. Triples with 45 and stolen bases with 115

13. Texas Rangers in 1980

14. The Mets won 145 games under Harrelson's tenure as manager.

15. Mike Cubbage

16. Lindy McDaniel

17. Jerry Grote and Cleon Jones

Keith Hernandez

1. "Mex"

2. 40th round

3. 11 Golden Gloves from 1978 to 1988

4. Doug Rau

5. Mike Scott

6. Willie Stargell

7. .344

8. Bud Harrelson

9. Rick Mahler (double in first inning), Jeff Dedmon (triple in fourth), Steve Shields (home run in eighth), and Terry Forster (single in twelfth)

10. Mike Phillips on June 25, 1976, against the Cubs

11. 18 in 1987

12. 1984 (.311), 1985 (.309), and 1986 (.310)

13. Jay Baller

14. Cleveland Indians

15. Todd Stottlemyre

16. Willie Crawford

Todd Hundley

1. Chris Donnels

2. Bruce Hurst

3. Bill Landrum

4. Jeff McKnight (Father Jim played for the Cubs in 1960 and 1962.)

5. Tim Spehr

6. Mackey Sasser

7. José Guzman

8. John Franco

9. 1996 (41) and 1997 (30)
10. Roy Campanella
11. Greg McMichael
12. Bernard Gilkey (1955)
13. Mickey Mantle and Ken Caminiti (1996)
14. Butch Huskey
15. Armando Benitez and Roger Cedeno
16. Jon Lieber
17. Five times: June 18, 1994; May 18, 1996; June 10, 1996; May 5, 1997; and July 30, 1997

Ron Hunt

1. Milwaukee Braves
2. Solly Hemus
3. .303
4. Bob Buhl
5. Pete Rose of the Cincinnati Reds
6. 10 (season high)
7. Dick Ellsworth
8. Ed Bailey
9. Phil Gagliano
10. Sandy Koufax
11. Woodie Fryman
12. 41 times
13. 50 in 1971
14. Tom Haller
15. Roy Face
16. Pete Richert was the pitcher, and Doug Camilli was the catcher.
17. The St. Louis Cardinals

Al Jackson

1. Jack Hamilton (1938), Dennis Musgraves (1943), Rickey Henderson (1958), and Tom O'Malley (1960)
2. Pittsburgh Pirates
3. 13, a career high
4. Willie Stargell
5. Warren Spahn of the Milwaukee Braves
6. "Little Al"
7. Charlie Smith
8. 43 wins

9. Jack Lamabe

10. Bob Gibson

11. Cincinnati Reds

12. 1962 and 1965

13. 561 strikeouts

14. Jack Hamilton

15. Jackson wore number 15 from 1962 to 1965 and number 38 from 1968 to 1969

16. Jay Hook (twice): July 19, 1962, and May 8, 1963; Dennis Ribant on August 17, 1964; and Tracy Stallard on September 16, 1964

Howard Johnson

1. "Hojo"

2. Sparky Anderson

3. Pete Redfern

4. Three: 1987 (36 homers, 32 stolen bases); 1989 (36 homers, 41 stolen bases); 1991 (38 homers, 30 stolen bases)

5. Ryne Sandberg (Chicago) and Will Clark (San Francisco)

6. .287 in 1989

7. Mo Sanford and Norm Charlton

8. 38 home runs and 117 RBIs

9. Will Clark (San Francisco) and Barry Bonds (Pittsburgh)

10. Darryl Strawberry

11. Bernard Gilkey

12. Wayne Garrett (709 games), Hubie Brooks (516 games), and Edgardo Alfonzo (515 games)

13. Mike Campbell

14. Chicago Cubs

15. Rip Collins

Cleon Jones

1. Duke Carmel

2. Bob Friend

3. Mark Carreon and Ricky Henderson

4. George Stone

5. Ron Brand

6. Pete Rose (Cincinnati), .348; and Roberto Clemente (Pittsburgh), .345

7. In 1971, Jones finished with a .319 batting average.

8. 23 games

9. Ken Forsch

10. Phil Linz
11. Jim Rooker
12. George Theodore and Rusty Staub
13. 93 home runs
14. Chicago White Sox
15. Ron Hunt in 1964 with a .303 batting average

Dave Kingman

1. University of Southern California
2. Dave Giusti
3. Houston Astros
4. 442 home runs
5. Steve Carlton
6. Phil Niekro
7. 7 multi–home run games
8. California Angels and New York Yankees
9. Pete Falcone (two) and Neil Allen
10. Steve Henderson
11. 37 home runs
12. Oakland A's
13. 35 home runs
14. 48 homers
15. .288
16. Charlie Fox
17. Dick Allen

Jerry Koosman

1. 12 (1967–1978)
2. 2.08
3. Grover Cleveland Alexander of the 1911 Philadelphia Phillies
4. Dodgers on April 11, 1968 (4–0) and Giants on April 17, 1968 (3–0)
5. Bill Hands
6. 19 victories in 1968
7. Johnny Bench (Bench narrowly won, 10½ to 9½ .)
8. John Bateman
9. Jose Pagan
10. 15 in a 10-inning game against San Diego on May 28, 1969
11. Tug McGraw
12. Jack Billingham was the pitcher, and Bill Plummer was the catcher.
13. Randy Jones

14. Ken Reitz
15. Ray Burris
16. Tom Seaver
17. Paul Owens
18. Frank Viola in 1990 (20–12)

Ed Kranepool

1. 18 years from 1962 to 1979
2. James Monroe High School
3. Hank Greenberg
4. $85,000
5. Don Elston
6. 16 home runs
7. 1965, but he did not participate in the game
8. Joe Kerrigan
9. 118
10. Bob Shaw
11. 90
12. 1974 with a .486 average (17 hits in 35 at bats) and 1977 with a .448 clip (13 for 29)
13. 1,304 games
14. Steve Stone
15. Stan Bahnsen
16. Mardie Cornejo
17. Ron Hodges
18. Roy McMillan
19. Jim Bethke

Al Leiter

1. Juan Nieves
2. Jesse Barfield
3. Tony Fernandez and John Olerud
4. 1996 and 2000
5. Eric Young
6. Jay Powell
7. Dennis Cook
8. 17 wins
9. Dwight Gooden
10. Derek Jeter
11. Damon Buford

12. 15 K's on August 1, 1999, at Wrigley Field
13. Greg Maddux
14. Gary Carter
15. Barry Larkin
16. Mike Piazza

Jon Matlack

1. Trumpbour
2. Milt Pappas
3. Steve Carlton
4. Roberto Clemente
5. John Milner
6. Marty Perez
7. Tommy Helms
8. 205 strikeouts
9. Ron Darling (1986)
10. Richie Zisk
11. Buzz Capra
12. Phil Niekro
13. 17 hits
14. 82 wins
15. The Detroit Tigers
16. Bud Harrelson and Rusty Staub
17. Ron Blomberg

Willie Mays

1. Warren Spahn
2. Birmingham Black Barons
3. Wes Westrum and George Bamberger
4. Don Mueller
5. Lance Johnson, who had 21 triples
6. 1956 (40), 1957 (38), 1958 (31), and 1959 (27)
7. 39 (He ranks fifth on the most home runs by Met opponents list.)
8. 141 RBIs
9. Jay Hook
10. Felipe Alou (.316) and Harvey Kuenn (.304)
11. George Foster
12. Charlie Williams
13. Don Carrithers
14. Jim Barr

15. 1979
16. Hack Wilson
17. Ed Bressoud
18. Davey Williams
19. Leo Durocher and Bill Rigney
20. Bobby Thomson
21. Hoyt Wilhelm
22. Carl Erskine
23. Larry Jackson
24. Orlando Cepeda, Willie McCovey, Gaylord Perry, and Duke Snider
25. Jesus Alou, Bob Hendley, Ron Herbel, Chuck Hiller, Ken MacKenzie, Bob Shaw, and Duke Snider

Lee Mazzilli
1. Welterweight
2. "The Italian Stallion" from the *Rocky* movies
3. Lincoln High School
4. Speed skating
5. Darold Knowles
6. Bruce Boisclair
7. Kent Tekulve
8. Larry Christenson
9. Tommy John and Charlie Hough
10. Dan Norman
11. Lenny Randle
12. .303
13. Al Hrabosky
14. 41 in 1980
15. Tim Burke
16. Toronto Blue Jays
17. Wally Schang
18. Don Robinson

Tug McGraw
1. Frank
2. Slapping his glove against his leg
3. Ray Washburn
4. Bob Friend
5. Jim McAndrew
6. Ron Taylor

7. 11 wins in 1971
8. Carl Morton
9. 1971 and 1972
10. Joe Morgan
11. Carl Morton
12. Don Hahn and Dave Schneck
13. 86 saves
14. Willie Wilson
15. Jim Bethke
16. Jerry Koosman
17. Ralph Terry
18. Orlando Cepeda

Felix Millan

1. Bob Bolin
2. Sammy Ellis
3. Gaylord Perry
4. Joe Morgan of Houston against the Milwaukee Braves
5. Sandy Vance
6. Danny Frisella and Gary Gentry
7. 1975
8. Roy McMillan
9. Father: Diego Segui; son: David Segui
10. 14 times in 585 plate appearances
11. Lance Johnson with 227 hits
12. Tommie Agee with 182 in 1970
13. Rusty Staub in 1973
14. Gary Carter
15. Ed Ott
16. The Taiyo Whales

John Olerud

1. Washington State University
2. Dave Winfield
3. Pete Harnisch
4. 54
5. .363
6. Robert Person
7. Montreal
8. Jose Vizcaino

9. .354

10. Dave Magadan

11. Felix Millan, 162 games in 1975; and Robin Ventura, 161 games in 1999

12. Bob Watson in 1977 with the Houston Astros and in 1979 with the Boston Red Sox

13. Dale Sveum

14. Barry Bonds

15. Eddie Murray

16. Fred Hutchinson

17. The Angels

Rey Ordonez

1. Cuba

2. Rick Honeycutt

3. Royce Clayton

4. 14 games

5. Rich Hunter

6. 37 at bats

7. Barry Larkin of Cincinnati

8. Cal Ripken Jr. from April 14 to July 27, 1990

9. Carlton Loewer

10. F. P. Santangelo

11. Numbers 0 and 10

12. Todd Zeile

13. Mike Bordick and Kurt Abbott

14. Al Moran (1963), Rod Gaspar (1969), and Kelvin Chapman (1979)

15. José Vizcaino

Jesse Orosco

1. Kent Tekulve (1,050 games), Hoyt Wilhelm (1,018), and Lee Smith (1,016)

2. Ben Oglivie

3. Craig Anderson in 1962 and Willard Hunter in 1964

4. Jim Bibby

5. Dwight Gooden and Tom Gorman

6. Tug McGraw in 1972

7. Roger McDowell

8. Tony Perez

9. Kevin Bass

10. Marty Barrett

11. Tommy Herr
12. 107 saves
13. Joe McEwing
14. The Indians, Brewers, and Orioles
15. Jim Kaat
16. Bill Buckner
17. Steve Carlton

Mike Piazza

1. 62d round
2. Steve Reed
3. Mike Scioscia
4. Benito Santiago of the San Diego Padres
5. Greg McMichael
6. Tommy LaSorda
7. Fred Lynn
8. Bill Dickey of the New York Yankees
9. Eric Karros (1992), Raul Mondesi (1994), Hideo Nomo (1995), and Todd Hollandsworth (1996)
10. Jeff Juden
11. Matt Franco
12. Jason Schmidt
13. Pittsburgh Pirates
14. Trevor Hoffman
15. George Foster (99), Bobby Bonilla (95), John Milner (94), and Cleon Jones (93)
16. Todd Zeile
17. Ted Williams
18. Carlos Almanzar
19. Ramon Martinez from the Dominican Republic on July 14, 1995, against Florida and Hideo Nomo from Japan on September 17, 1996, against Colorado
20. Alberto Castillo (22 games), Tim Spehr (15), Rick Wilkins (4), Todd Pratt (2), and Jim Tatum (1)
21. Odalis Perez
22. Derek Lowe
23. Mike Hampton
24. Terry Mulholland
25. Steve Karsay

AMAZING METS TRIVIA

Rick Reed

1. Keith Hernandez had two singles, and Mookie Wilson had the other single.
2. Bobby Bonilla
3. Buffalo
4. Kansas City Royals, Texas Rangers, and Cincinnati Reds
5. Greg Maddux
6. Pete Schourek
7. Steve Trachsel
8. 1997 with 10 and 1999 with 11
9. 1998 and 2001
10. Wade Boggs
11. Edgar Renteria
12. Roger Cedeno
13. Robert Person
14. Jim Leyland
15. Matt Lawton
16. 16 wins
17. The outfielder is Darren Reed, and the relief pitcher is Steve Reed.
18. Francisco Cordova

Tom Seaver

1. "The Franchise" and "Tom Terrific"
2. William D. Eckert
3. Philadelphia Phillies and Cleveland Indians
4. Solly Hemus
5. Bill Denehy
6. Dick Selma
7. Wes Westrum
8. Curt Simmons
9. Dick Hughes of the St. Louis Cardinals
10. Jack Sanford
11. Juan Pizarro
12. Ferguson Jenkins
13. Fernando Valenzuela
14. Phil Niekro
15. Walter Johnson and Rube Waddell
16. Willie Montanez
17. Manny Sanguillen

18. 1969, 1973, and 1975

19. George Hendrick

20. Don Werner

21. Jimmy Qualls on July 9, 1969; Mike Compton on May 15, 1970; Vic Davalillo on September 26, 1971; Leron Lee on July 4, 1972; and Steve Ontiveros on April 17, 1977

22. Jack Hamilton

23. Dan Driessen

24. Five times: 1970 (283), 1971 (289), 1973 (251), 1975 (243), and 1976 (235)

25. Keith Hernandez

26. Lloyd McClendon, who was named the skipper for the Pittsburgh Pirates for the 2001 season

27. Doug Sisk

28. 198 games

29. Don Baylor

30. Joe Cowley

31. Neil Allen

32. Art Howe

33. 1988

34. Hal Newhouser

35. Woodie Fryman

36. Chuck Estrada

37. Rich Nye

38. Craig Swan

39. Steve Lyons

40. 3,640 strikeouts

41. Frank Viola

Rusty Staub

1. Daniel

2. "Le Grande Orange"

3. Don Drysdale

4. Bill Stoneman

5. Tim Foli, Mike Jorgensen, and Ken Singleton

6. Dock Ellis

7. Sam McDowell

8. George Stone

9. Dan Driessen

10. 8

11. Clint Hurdle

12. Rick Rhoden

13. Jeff Reardon

14. Bud Harrelson

15. 1979

16. Mickey Lolich

17. Robin Roberts, who was inducted in 1976, Joe Morgan (1990), and Nellie Fox (1997)

John Stearns

1. "Dude"

2. University of Colorado

3. Defensive back

4. David Clyde

5. Buffalo Bills

6. Mike Torrez

7. Del Unser and Mac Scarce

8. Ray Burris

9. Woodie Fryman

10. Ken Sanders

11. Bill Robinson

12. Johnny Kling

13. Jason Kendall

14. Dave Concepcion

15. 2000 and 2001

16. Mike Fitzgerald (107 games), Ron Hodges (35), Junior Ortiz (32), and John Gibbons (9)

Darryl Strawberry

1. Crenshaw High School

2. Billy Beane

3. George Bamberger

4. Ben Hayes

5. Lee Tunnell

6. .284 in 1987

7. Howard Johnson

8. Juan Eichelberger

9. 1988 with 39 home runs

10. John Franco

11. 252 home runs

12. Eric Davis
13. Jose Vizcaino
14. Ken Dayley
15. Jason Jacome
16. Juan Samuel

Craig Swan

1. Arizona State University
2. Rusty Staub, Cleon Jones, and Don Hahn
3. Ed Halicki
4. Andy Messersmith
5. Willie Crawford
6. Steve Rogers
7. Pete Rose
8. Jerry Turner
9. Ron Hodges
10. Ferguson Jenkins
11. 59 wins
12. Mike Scott
13. California Angels
14. 1979 (14–13) and 1982 (11–7)
15. Dick Ruthven

Ron Swoboda

1. University of Maryland
2. Turk Farrell
3. 19 home runs
4. .281 in 1967
5. "Rocky"
6. Crosley Field
7. Mike Kekich
8. Chuck Hartenstein
9. Brooks Robinson
10. Cleon Jones
11. Don Hahn
12. 69 home runs
13. New York Yankees in 1973
14. Ferguson Jenkins
15. Whitey Kurowski was at Buffalo, while Ernie White was at Williamsport.

Robin Ventura

1. Oklahoma State
2. Jack McDowell
3. Seoul, Korea
4. Ben McDonald
5. Roger Clemens
6. Nolan Ryan
7. Graig Nettles of the New York Yankees
8. Frank Robinson
9. Ray Durham (2B) and Frank Thomas (1B)
10. Brooks Robinson (16) and Buddy Bell (6)
11. Rick Cerone
12. Jim Abbott and Horacio Estrada
13. Chris Holt
14. David Justice
15. 16
16. Alberto Castillo, Tony Tarasco, and David Weathers
17. Howard Johnson, Kevin McReynolds, and John Milner
18. Jeff Torborg

Mookie Wilson

1. William
2. University of South Carolina
3. John Curtis
4. Nino Espinosa
5. 1984
6. Clint Hurdle
7. Ray Knight
8. Sid Bream
9. Tom Glavine
10. 281 steals
11. 62 triples
12. Bruce Sutter
13. The Toronto Blue Jays
14. 1996
15. Steve Henderson was in left field; Claudell Washington was in right field.
16. Shane Rawley
17. Keith Miller
18. Gary Lucas

METS TRIVIA: The Managers

Yogi Berra

1. Johnny Neun
2. Early Wynn
3. Allie Reynolds
4. Joe Garagiola and Bobby Hofman
5. Phil Regan
6. Moe Drabowsky
7. Johnny Keane
8. Jim Bethke
9. Ray Herbert and Gary Wagner
10. Roy McMillan
11. Tony Cloninger
12. Phil Lombardi, Hal Reniff, and Roy Staiger
13. Ed Kranepool
14. 71 hits
15. Joe McCarthy
16. Clem Labine (Duke Snider is fourth, born a month later on September 19, 1926.)
17. The Houston Astros
18. Joe DiMaggio, Whitey Ford, Johnny Mize, and Phil Rizzuto
19. Sandy Amoros (LF), Pee Wee Reese (SS), and Gil Hodges (1B)
20. Gil McDougald
21. Don Baylor and Lou Piniella
22. Roy McMillan, Bud Harrelson, Mike Cubbage, and Bobby Valentine
23. 1951, 1954, and 1955
24. Spud Chandler
25. Bobby Brown, M.D.
26. Sheriff Robinson

Gil Hodges

1. Leo Durocher
2. Hank Borowy
3. Bobby Bragan
4. Fritz Ostermuller
5. Rex Barney
6. Johnny Antonelli
7. Carl Furillo
8. 7 years (1949–1955)

9. Larry Jackson
10. Dick Ellsworth
11. Elio Chacon (SS) and Felix Mantilla (2B)
12. Ray Sadecki
13. Billy Pierce
14. Charlie Neal
15. Mickey Vernon
16. Robin Roberts
17. Ken Singleton
18. Jesus Alou
19. Jim Lemon
20. Joe Pignatano, Rube Walker, and Eddie Yost
21. Roy Campanella and Pee Wee Reese
22. Elston Howard
23. Chuck Klein
24. Bill White
25. Ed Kranepool, Al Jackson, and Bob Aspromonte

Davey Johnson

1. Jerry Adair
2. Jim McGlothlin
3. Andy Etchebarren, Sam Bowens, and Boog Powell
4. Clyde Wright
5. 1969–1971
6. Johnny Oates
7. Phil Hennigan
8. Tom Hall
9. Rogers Hornsby
10. Darrell Evans (41 home runs) and Henry Aaron (40)
11. Frank Howard
12. Randy Myers
13. 595 victories
14. Cincinnati Reds and Los Angeles Dodgers
15. Bud Harrelson
16. Hank Bauer
17. Steve Barber
18. Jim Hannan
19. Mark Belanger
20. Denny McLain
21. Bob Shirley

22. Jay Johnstone
23. Chicago Cubs
24. Tommie Agee, then of the Chicago White Sox
25. Al Lopez

Casey Stengel

1. 9 home runs in 1920
2. Jack Dalton (CF, .319) and Zack Wheat (LF, .319)
3. George Burns
4. Bill Doak
5. Joe Bush
6. Hy Myers
7. Dave Bancroft
8. Jesse Haines
9. 1934–1936
10. 1955 (Brooklyn), 1957 (Milwaukee), and 1960 (Pittsburgh)
11. Joe McCarthy in 1932, 1936, 1937, 1938, 1939, 1941, and 1943
12. Bucky Harris
13. Ralph Houk
14. Wes Westrum
15. 175 games
16. Warren Spahn
17. Johnny Lewis
18. Ted Williams
19. Tug McGraw
20. Bill Dahlen
21. Lee Walls
22. Yogi Berra, Jesse Gonder, Tom Sturdivant, Marv Throneberry, and Gene Woodling
23. Charles Dillon
24. Claude Hendrix
25. Willie McCovey of San Francisco on July 30, 1959, and Kirby Puckett of Minnesota on May 8, 1984

Joe Torre

1. Del Crandall
2. Joey Jay
3. Billy Williams
4. Mack Jones (31), Felipe Alou (23), and Gene Oliver (21)
5. 30 home runs

6. Tom Seaver

7. Orlando Cepeda

8. Bud Harrelson (SS), Al Weis (2B), and Donn Clendenon (1B)

9. 230 hits

10. Felix Millan

11. Casey Stengel (37 wins), Joe McCarthy (30), John McGraw (26), Connie Mack (24), and Walter Alston (20)

12. Bob Apodaca

13. Solly Hemus

14. Casey Stengel, Yogi Berra, and Dallas Green

15. Roy Campanella

16. The California Angels

17. Whitey Herzog (80 games) and Red Schoendienst (24 games)

18. Joe Frazier

19. Chuck Dressen

20. Bob Veale

21. Mike Jorgensen

22. Harvey Haddix

23. Lou Gehrig (493), Carl Yastrzemski (452), Rocky Colavito (374), and Hank Greenberg (331)

24. Juan Marichal

25. Lou Brock, Steve Carlton, Bob Gibson, Phil Niekro, Red Schoendienst, and Tom Seaver

Bobby Valentine

1. Spokane, the AAA affiliate of the Los Angeles Dodgers

2. Tommy LaSorda

3. Steve Renko

4. Dick Green

5. .274 in 1972 (119 games)

6. Paul Siebert

7. Phil Niekro

8. Seattle Mariners

9. Doug Rader

10. Kevin Kennedy

11. Bud Harrelson

12. Chiba Lotte Marines

13. Dallas Green

14. 536 victories

15. Tim Foli

16. Jim Lefebvre
17. Milt Wilcox
18. Frank Robinson
19. The Cincinnati Reds
20. Pat Zachry
21. Bruce Bochy, Larry Bowa, Ron Gardenhire, and Clint Hurdle
22. Dave Roberts
23. Glendon Rusch
24. Ralph Branca
25. Mike Bruhert

POSTSEASON YEARS

1969
1. Don Shaw
2. Rich Nye
3. Bud Harrelson
4. Gaylord Perry
5. Ferguson Jenkins
6. 9½ games
7. Ken Boswell
8. Jerry Koosman and Don Cardwell
9. Steve Carlton
10. Art Shamsky
11. Gary Gentry
12. Donn Clendenon, who had two homers, and Ed Charles
13. Tony Gonzalez, who grounded out to third baseman Wayne Garrett
14. Infielders Bob Aspromonte and Felix Millan and pitcher George Stone
15. Al Weis
16. Elrod Hendricks and Paul Blair
17. Dave Leonhard in game 3, on October 14, 1969
18. Andy Etchebarren
19. Ron Taylor
20. Jack DiLauro, Cal Koonce, Jim McAndrew, and Tug McGraw
21. Bobby Pfeil
22. Jim "Mudcat" Grant
23. Lou DiMuro

1973
1. Steve Carlton
2. "You Gotta Believe!"
3. Ron Hodges

4. George Theodore was the left fielder, and Don Hahn was in center field.

5. Don Gullett

6. Tim McCarver

7. Third baseman Wayne Garrett was the relay man and Ron Hodges was the catcher.

8. 12 games

9. Rusty Staub

10. Glenn Beckert popped out to first baseman John Milner, who stepped on first base to complete a double play.

11. Andy Kosco

12. Ross Grimsley and Tom Hall

13. Buzz Capra of New York and Pedro Borbon of the Reds

14. Bert Campaneris

15. Billy Conigliaro

16. John Milner

17. Pete Rose in the eighth inning and Johnny Bench in the ninth inning

18. Rusty Staub and Don Hahn

1986

1. Bruce Berenyi (7), Rick Anderson (5), John Mitchell (1), and Randy Niemann (1)

2. Gary Carter

3. Kevin Mitchell

4. Bobby Ojeda

5. Tim Teufel

6. Gary Carter, Darryl Strawberry, and Kevin Mitchell

7. Chico Walker

8. Luis Rivera

9. Glenn Davis

10. Dave Smith

11. Charlie Kerfeld

12. Mike Scott

13. Joe Sambito and Calvin Schiraldi

14. Dennis "Oil Can" Boyd

15. Ed Hearn as catcher and Randy Niemann as pitcher

16. Ray Knight

17. Mike Krukow

18. Dave Magadan

19. Dennis Eckersley

20. Howard Johnson, who was playing shortstop

1988

1. Kevin Elster and Lenny Dykstra
2. Damon Berryhill
3. Bob McClure was signed as a free agent, and Edwin Nunez was acquired by trade.
4. Kevin McReynolds
5. Glenn Davis
6. 152 home runs
7. Ron Darling
8. Don Carman
9. Lance Parrish
10. Darryl Strawberry and Gary Carter
11. Jay Howell
12. John Shelby
13. David Cone
14. Gregg Jefferies and Darryl Strawberry
15. Tim Leary (1981, 1983–1984) and Alejandro Pena (1990–1991)
16. St. Petersburg, Florida

1999

1. Orel Hershiser and Al Leiter
2. Curt Schilling
3. Hubie Brooks
4. Roger Clemens
5. 68 errors
6. Matt Franco
7. Rickey Henderson scored the tying run, and Edgardo Alfonzo scored the winning run.
8. Kenny Rogers
9. Steve Parris
10. Edgardo Alfonzo against Bobby Chouinard in game 1 of the 1999 National League Division Series
11. Tony Womack
12. Matt Mantei
13. Octavio Dotel
14. Kevin McGlinchy
15. Gerald Williams
16. Shawon Dunston
17. Brad Clontz

2000

1. Benny Agbayani
2. Derek Bell
3. Mike Piazza
4. Melvin Mora
5. Ray Grimes
6. Jeff Kent
7. Aaron Fultz
8. Barry Bonds
9. Rick Wilkins
10. 1956, when the Yankees beat the Brooklyn Dodgers in seven games
11. José Vizcaino
12. Todd Zeile
13. John Franco
14. Orlando "El Duque" Hernandez
15. Jeff Nelson in game 2 and Denny Neagle in game 4
16. Todd Zeile
17. Mike Stanton

MISCELLANEOUS METS TRIVIA

1962 Original Mets

1. Frank Thomas
2. Marvin Eugene Throneberry
3. Ken MacKenzie (5–4)
4. Joey Amalfitano
5. Charlie Neal, who batted third and played second base, and Don Zimmer, who hit seventh and was at third base
6. Tom Sturdivant (1964) and Dick Stuart (1966)
7. Sherman "Roadblock" Jones
8. 4
9. Bob Friend
10. Dallas Green
11. Hobie Landrith, Gil Hodges
12. 17 games
13. Felix Mantilla
14. Rod Kanehl
15. Red Kress (November 29, 1962) and Roger Hornsby (January 5, 1963)

16. Charlie Neal (Atlanta Black Crackers) and Choo Choo Coleman (Indianapolis Clowns)

17. Sammy Drake (Solly) and Marv Throneberry (Faye)

18. Chris Cannizzaro, Jim Hickman, and Bob L. Miller

Uniform Numbers

1. Jim Beauchamp
2. Hideo Nomo, Derek Bell, and David Cone
3. Number 37 worn by manager Casey Stengel
4. Ron Swoboda and Ken Boyer
5. 99 by Turk Wendell
6. Lee Mazzilli and John Stearns
7. Kevin Collins and Bobby Pfeil
8. Rick Baldwin
9. Butch Huskey
10. Number 51
11. Number 13
12. Kelvin Torve and Rickey Henderson
13. John Franco (He switched to number 45.)
14. Clem Labine, Grover Powell, Jim Bethke, and Gordon Richardson
15. Jonathan Hurst
16. Numbers 44 (1983–1984), 12 (1985–1989), and 15 (1989–1991)
17. Pat Howell
18. Mark Clark
19. 1969: Donn Clendenon; 1986: Ray Knight, uniform number 22
20. Terry McDaniel

Trades

1. Tom Parsons
2. Dave Mlicki
3. Frank Viola
4. Dean Chance
5. Neil Allen and Rick Ownbey
6. Greg Field
7. José Cardenal
8. Tom Grieve, Ken Henderson, and Willie Montanez
9. Bob Ojeda
10. Walt Terrell
11. Frank Tanana
12. Mark Clark, Manny Alexander, and Lance Johnson

13. Rick White and Bubba Trammell
14. Mike Phillips
15. Tommy Davis
16. Preston Wilson, Ed Yarnall, and Geoff Goetz
17. Bob Aspromonte
18. Richie Hebner

Rookies

1. Ron Hunt
2. Dick Rusteck
3. Tsuyoshi Shinjo
4. Derek Wallace
5. Tim Leary
6. Steve Henderson
7. Les Rohr
8. Alex Ochoa
9. Butch Huskey
10. Mike Vail
11. Dave Schneck
12. Randy Tate
13. Jim McAndrew
14. Rob Gardner
15. Pete Schourek
16. Jim Hickman
17. Dick Selma
18. Steve Bieser
19. Johnny Stephenson
20. Ted Schreiber
21. John Milner

Nicknames

1. Richie Ashburn
2. Larry Burright
3. Ed Charles
4. Donn Clendenon
5. Choo Choo (Clarence) Coleman
6. Kevin Collins
7. Jack Fisher
8. Ed Glynn
9. Tom Hall

10. Jack Hamilton
11. Lance Johnson
12. Rod Kanehl
13. Jim McAndrew
14. Duke Snider
15. Dick Stuart
16. George Theodore
17. Rusty Tillman
18. Frank Viola
19. Eddie Yost
20. Anthony Young
21. Jason Isringhausen, Bill Pulsipher, and Paul Wilson
22. Chuck Hiller
23. Frank Howard
24. Don Zimmer

All-Stars

1. Richie Ashburn
2. Dean Chance
3. Johnny Callison
4. Don Drysdale
5. Carl Yastrzemski
6. Cleon Jones
7. Lance Parrish, Chet Lemon, and Alvin Davis
8. 1970
9. Sparky Lyle
10. Bill Madlock
11. Pat Zachry
12. Jim Kern
13. Ron Guidry
14. Don Mattingly
15. Gary Carter, Dwight Gooden, Keith Hernandez, and Darryl Strawberry
16. Frank Viola
17. 1968

Record Holders

1. Ty Cobb
2. Mark Carreon
3. Dick Smith
4. Benny Agbayani

5. Jack Fisher

6. Rusty Staub in 1974

7. Joe Torre

8. John Olerud

9. Larry Elliot, Ron Swoboda, Lee Mazzilli, Dave Kingman, Bobby Bonilla, Mike Piazza (who did it twice), and Edgardo Alfonzo

10. Butch Huskey

11. 35 home runs

12. San Diego Padres

13. Al Ferrara

14. Dave Kingman with 8 RBIs on June 4, 1976, against Los Angeles

15. Ron Swoboda (June 22, 1969, game 1), Frank Taveras (May 1, 1979), Dave Kingman (May 28, 1982), and Ryan Thompson (September 29, 1993)

16. Pete Falcone

17. Mickey Morandini

Two-Term Mets

1. Frank Lary

2. Bill Almon

3. Bobby Bonilla

4. Hubie Brooks

5. Tim Foli

6. Lenny Harris

7. Clint Hurdle

8. Mike Jorgensen

9. Terry Leach

10. Greg McMichael

11. Kevin McReynolds

12. Ray Sadecki

13. Rusty Staub

14. Alex Trevino

15. Ricky Trlicek

16. Roger Cedeno

17. Bob L. Miller, who returned in 1973 after leaving following the 1962 season; and David Cone who returned in 2003 after leaving in 1992

Hall of Fame Opponents

1. Willie Stargell (60), Mike Schmidt (49), Willie McCovey (48), and Hank Aaron (45)

2. Gaylord Perry

3. Jim Bunning
4. Willie Stargell
5. Stan Musial
6. Bill Mazeroski
7. Steve Carlton
8. Orlando Cepeda
9. Willie McCovey
10. Johnny Bench
11. Ernie Banks
12. Roberto Clemente
13. Billy Williams
14. Bob Gibson
15. Juan Marichal
16. Jim Palmer
17. Frank Robinson
18. Sandy Koufax
19. Rollie Fingers, Catfish Hunter, and Reggie Jackson

Ralph Kiner

1. Rosy Rowswell (1936–1954) and Bob Prince (1948–1975)
2. Kiner's Korner
3. 369 home runs
4. Babe Ruth
5. Vern Stephens
6. .313 in 1947
7. Johnny Mize
8. Tommy Leach
9. Larry Jansen
10. Hank Greenberg
11. Paul Waner
12. The Brooklyn Dodgers
13. Ted Williams
14. Cliff Chambers
15. Al Corwin
16. Catcher Joe Garagiola, outfielder "Catfish" Metkovich, and pitcher Howie Pollett
17. Branch Rickey
18. Frank Thomas (1951–1953), Gene Woodling (1947), and Gus Bell (1950–1952)

19. Willie Stargell
20. Frankie Baumholz (CF) and Hank Sauer (RF)
21. The Cleveland Indians
22. The San Diego Padres
23. The Chicago White Sox
24. 1975
25. Billy Herman
26. Number 4

Lindsey Nelson

1. Multicolored sport jackets
2. Bill Stern
3. The Univeristy of Tennessee
4. Harry Walker
5. The Liberty Broadcast System
6. Gordon McLendon
7. Leo Durocher
8. Red Grange
9. The University of Notre Dame
10. Paul Hornung
11. The Houston Astrodome
12. *Backstage at the Mets*
13. Brent Musberger
14. Frank Gifford
15. WJRZ 970
16. The San Francisco Giants
17. Steve Albert
18. The Cotton Bowl
19. The Mutual Broadcast System
20. General William C. Westmoreland
21. Tom Seaver's 300th career victory
22. 1988

Bob Murphy

1. The *San Diego Union*
2. The U.S. Marines
3. The University of Tulsa
4. The University of Oklahoma
5. The Boston Red Sox

6. Curt Gowdy

7. The Baltimore Orioles

8. WABC 770

9. Monte Irvin

10. Merle Harmon

11. Orange Bowl (six times) and Gator Bowl (five times)

12. Steve LaMar

13. Gary Thorne

14. WHN 1050

15. Gary Cohen

16. Ed Coleman

17. 1994

18. "We'll be back with the happy recap in just a moment."

METS ALL-TIME RECORDS

Individual Career Batting

Games:	Ed Kranepool, 1,853
At bats:	Ed Kranepool, 5,436
Runs:	Darryl Strawberry, 662
Hits:	Ed Kranepool, 1,418
Doubles:	Ed Kranepool, 225
Triples:	Mookie Wilson, 62
Home runs:	Darryl Strawberry, 252
RBIs:	Darryl Strawberry, 733
Total bases:	Ed Kranepool, 2,047
Stolen bases:	Mookie Wilson, 281
Sacrifice flies:	Ed Kranepool, 58
Strikeouts:	Darryl Strawberry, 960
Walks:	Darryl Strawberry, 580
Hit by pitch	Ron Hunt, 41
Batting average:	John Olerud, .315
Slugging average:	Mike Piazza, .581
Pinch hits:	Ed Kranepool, 90
Pinch homers:	Mark Carreon, 8
Grand slams:	Mike Piazza, 6

Individual Season Batting

Games:	Felix Millan, 162 (1975); John Olerud, 162 (1999)
At bats:	Lance Johnson, 682 (1996)
Runs:	Edgardo Alfonzo, 123 (1999)
Hits:	Lance Johnson, 227 (1996)
Doubles:	Bernard Gilkey, 44 (1996)
Triples:	Lance Johnson, 21 (1996)
Home runs:	Todd Hundley, 41 (1996)
RBIs:	Mike Piazza, 124 (1999)
Total bases:	Lance Johnson, 327 (1996)
Stolen bases:	Roger Cedeno, 66 (1999)

Sacrifice flies:	Gary Carter, 15 (1986), Howard Johnson, 15 (1991)
Strikeouts:	Tommie Agee, 156 (1970), Dave Kingman, 156 (1982)
Walks:	John Olerud, 125 (1999)
Hit by pitch	Ron Hunt, 13 (1963), John Olerud, 13 (1997)
Batting average:	John Olerud, .354 (1998)
Slugging average:	Mike Piazza, .614 (2000)
Pinch hits:	Rusty Staub, 24 (1983)
Pinch homers:	Danny Heep, 4 (1983), Mark Carreon, 4 (1989)
Grand slams:	John Milner, 3 (1976), Robin Ventura, 3 (1999), Mike Piazza, 3 (2000)
Hitting streak:	Hubie Brooks, 24 games (1984), Mike Piazza, 24 games (1999)

Individual Game Batting

At bats: (25 innings)	Dave Schneck, 11, September 11, 1974, versus St. Louis
Runs:	Edgardo Alfonzo, 6, August 30, 1999, at Houston
Hits:	Edgardo Alfonzo, 6, August 30, 1999 at Houston
Doubles:	3 by 18 players
	Last: Edgardo Alfonzo, April 18, 2000, versus Milwaukee
Triples:	Doug Flynn, 3, August 5, 1980, at Montreal
Home runs:	Jim Hickman, 3, September 3, 1965, at St. Louis
	Dave Kingman, 3, June 4, 1976, at Los Angeles
	Claudell Washington, 3, June 22, 1980, at Los Angeles
	Darryl Strawberry, 3, August 5, 1985, at Chicago
	Gary Carter, 3, September 3, 1985, at San Diego
	Edgardo Alfonzo, 3, August 30, 1999, at Houston
RBIs:	Dave Kingman, 8, June 4, 1976, at Los Angeles
Total bases:	Edgardo Alfonzo, 16, August 30, 1999, at Houston (3 HR, 1 2B, 2 1B)
Stolen bases:	Vince Coleman, 3, June 26, 1992, at St. Louis
	Vince Coleman, 3, June 23, 1993, versus Montreal
	Roger Cedeno, 3, May 14, 1999, at Philadelphia
Strikeouts:	Ron Swoboda, 5, June 22, 1969, versus St. Louis (game 1)
	Frank Taveras, 5, May 1, 1979, versus San Diego
	Dave Kingman, 5, May 28, 1982, versus Houston
	Ryan Thompson, 5, September 29, 1993, versus St. Louis

AMAZING METS TRIVIA

| Walks: | Vince Coleman, 5, August 10, 1992, versus Pittsburgh (16 innings) |

Individual Career Pitching

Games:	John Franco, 605
Starts:	Tom Seaver, 395
Complete games:	Tom Seaver, 171
Innings:	Tom Seaver 3,045.0
Strikeouts:	Tom Seaver, 2,541
Walks:	Tom Seaver, 847
Wins:	Tom Seaver, 198
Losses:	Jerry Koosman, 137
Shutouts:	Tom Seaver, 44
Saves:	John Franco, 274
ERA:	Tom Seaver, 2.57

Individual Season Pitching

Games:	Turk Wendell, 80 (1999)
Starts:	Jack Fisher, 36 (1965), and Tom Seaver, 36 (1970, 1973, 1975)
Complete games:	Tom Seaver, 21 (1971)
Innings:	Tom Seaver, 290.2 (1970)
Strikeouts:	Tom Seaver, 289 (1971)
Walks:	Nolan Ryan, 116 (1971)
Wins:	Tom Seaver, 25 (1969)
Losses:	Roger Craig, 24 (1962), and Jack Fisher, 24 (1965)
Shutouts:	Dwight Gooden, 8 (1985)
Saves:	Armando Benitez, 43 (2001)
ERA:	Dwight Gooden, 1.53 (1985)

Individual Game Pitching

Innings:	Al Jackson, 15, August 14, 1962, versus Philadelphia
	Rob Gardner, 15, October 2, 1965, versus Philadelphia
Strikeouts:	Tom Seaver, 19, April 22, 1970, versus San Diego
	David Cone, 19, October 6, 1991, at Philadelphia
Walks:	Mike Torrez, 10, July 21, 1983, at Cincinnati

Team Season Records

Wins:	108 (1986)
Losses:	120 (1962)
Runs:	853 (1999)
Hits:	1,553 (1999)
Doubles:	297 (1999)
Triples:	47 (1978, 1996)
Home runs:	198 (2000)
Grand slams:	8 (1999, 2000)
Pinch homers:	12 (1983)
Stolen bases:	159 (1987)
Walks:	717 (1999)
Strikeouts:	1,203 (1968)
Hit by pitch:	65 (2001)
Batting average:	.279 (1999)
Slugging average:	.434 (1987, 1999)
Errors:	210 (1962, 1963)
Fewest errors:	68 (1999)
Double plays:	171 (1966, 1983)
Fielding average:	.989 (1999)
Attendance:	3,047,724 (1988)

Team Game Records

Runs:	23, August 16, 1987, at Chicago
Runs allowed:	26, June 11, 1985, at Philadelphia
Runs, inning:	10, June 12, 1979, sixth inning versus Cincinnati
	10, June 30, 2000, eighth inning versus Atlanta
Hits:	28, July 4, 1985, at Atlanta (19 innings)
Hits (nine innings):	23, May 26, 1964, at Chicago
	23, April 29, 2000, at Colorado
Home runs:	6, April 4, 1988, at Montreal
	6, June 15, 1999, at Cincinnati

METS SEASON BY SEASON

1962　40–162 10th place, 60.5 games behind San Francisco
Manager: Casey Stengel
Batting leader: Felix Mantilla, .275
Home run leader: Frank Thomas, 34
Leading winner: Roger Craig, 10–24
All-star: Richie Ashburn

1963　51–111 10th place, 48.5 games behind Los Angeles
Manager: Casey Stengel
Batting leader: Ron Hunt, .272
Home run leader: Jim Hickman, 17
Leading winner: Al Jackson, 13–17
All-star: Duke Snider

1964　53–109 10th place, 40 games behind St. Louis
Manager: Casey Stengel
Batting leader: Ron Hunt, .303
Home run leader: Charley Smith, 20
Leading winner: Al Jackson, 11–16
All-star: Ron Hunt (starting second baseman)

1965　50–112 10th place, 47 games behind Los Angeles
Manager: Casey Stengel, Wes Westrum
Batting leader: Ed Kranepool, .253
Home run leader: Ron Swoboda, 19
Leading winner: Al Jackson, 8–20; Jack Fisher, 8–24
All-star: Ed Kranepool

1966　66–95 9th place, 28.5 games behind Los Angeles
Manager: Wes Westrum
Batting leader: Ron Hunt, .288
Home run leader: Ed Kranepool, 16
Leading winner: Dennis Ribant, 11–9; Bob Shaw, 11–10; Jack
　　Fisher, 11–14
All-star: Ron Hunt

1967   61–101 10th place, 40.5 games behind St. Louis
Manager: Wes Westrum, Salty Parker
Batting leader: Tommy Davis, .302
Home run leader: Tommy Davis, 16
Leading winner: Tom Seaver, 16–13
All-star: Tom Seaver

1968   73-89 9th place, 24 games behind St. Louis
Manager: Gil Hodges
Batting leader: Cleon Jones, .297
Home run leader: Ed Charles, 15
Leading winner: Jerry Koosman, 19–12
All-stars: Jerry Grote (starting catcher), Tom Seaver, Jerry Koosman

1969   100-62 1st place, 8 games ahead of Chicago (East)
Defeated Atlanta, 3–0 in NLCS
Defeated Baltimore, 4–1 in World Series
Manager: Gil Hodges
Batting leader: Cleon Jones, .340
Home run leader: Tommie Agee, 26
Leading winner: Tom Seaver, 25–7
All-stars: Cleon Jones (starting outfielder), Tom Seaver, Jerry
     Koosman

1970   83–79 3rd place, 6 games behind Pittsburgh (East)
Manager: Gil Hodges
Batting leader: Tommie Agee, .286
Home run leader: Tommie Agee, 24
Leading winner: Tom Seaver, 18–12
All-stars: Gil Hodges (manager), Tom Seaver (starting pitcher),
     Bud Harrelson

1971   83–79 3rd place tie with Chicago, 14 games behind Pittsburgh (East)
Manager: Gil Hodges
Batting leader: Cleon Jones, .319
Home run leader: Tommie Agee, Cleon Jones, Ed Kranepool, 14
Leading winner: Tom Seaver, 20–10
All-stars: Bud Harrelson (starting shortstop), Tom Seaver

1972   83–73 3rd place, 13.5 games behind Pittsburgh (East)
Manager: Yogi Berra
Batting leader: Rusty Staub, .293

Home run leader: John Milner, 17
Leading winner: Tom Seaver, 21–12
All-stars: Willie Mays (starting outfielder), Tom Seaver, Tug McGraw

1973   82–79 1st place, 1.5 games ahead of St. Louis (East)
Defeated Cincinnati, 3–2 in NLCS
Lost to Oakland, 4–3 in World Series
Manager: Yogi Berra
Batting leader: Felix Millan, .290
Home run leader: John Milner, 23
Leading winner: Tom Seaver, 19–10
All-stars: Willie Mays, Tom Seaver

1974   71–91 5th place, 17 games behind Pittsburgh (East)
Manager: Yogi Berra
Batting leader: Cleon Jones, .282
Home run leader: John Milner, 20
Leading winner: Jerry Koosman, 15–11
All-stars: Yogi Berra (manager), Jerry Grote, Jon Matlack

1975   82–80 3rd place tie with St. Louis, 10.5 games behind Pittsburgh
(East)
Manager: Yogi Berra, Roy McMillan
Batting leader: Del Unser, .294
Home run leader: Dave Kingman, 36
Leading winner: Tom Seaver, 22–9
All-stars: Jon Matlack, Tom Seaver

1976   86–76 3rd place, 15 games behind Philadelphia (East)
Manager: Joe Frazier
Batting leader: Felix Millan, .282
Home runs: Dave Kingman, 37
Leading winner: Jerry Koosman, 21–10
All-stars: Dave Kingman (starting outfielder), Tom Seaver, Jon
Matlack

1977   64–98 6th place, 37 games behind Philadelphia (East)
Manager: Joe Frazier, Joe Torre
Batting leader: Len Randle, .304
Home run leader: Steve Henderson, John Milner, John Stearns, 12
Leading winner: Nino Espinosa, 10–13
All-star: John Stearns

1978   66–96 6th place, 24 games behind Philadelphia (East)
Manager: Joe Torre
Batting leader: Lee Mazzilli, .273
Home run leader: Willie Montanez, 17
Leading winner: Nino Espinosa, 11–15
All-star: Pat Zachry

1979   63–99 6th place, 35 games behind Pittsburgh (East)
Manager: Joe Torre
Batting leader: Lee Mazzilli, .303
Home run leader: Joel Youngblood, 16
Leading winner: Craig Swan, 14–13
All-Stars: Lee Mazzilli, John Stearns

1980   67–95 5th place, 24 games behind Philadelphia (East)
Manager: Joe Torre
Batting leader: Steve Henderson, .290
Home run leader, Lee Mazzilli, 16
Leading winner: Mark Bomback, 10–8
All-star: John Stearns

1981   41–62 Split season
17–34 5th place (1st half), 15 games behind Philadelphia (East)
24–28 4th place (2d half), 5.5 games behind Montreal (East)
Manager: Joe Torre
Batting leader: Hubie Brooks, .307
Home run leader: Dave Kingman, 22
Leading winner: Neil Allen 7–6, Pat Zachry, 7–14
All-star: Joel Youngblood

1982   65–97 6th place, 27 games behind St. Louis (East)
Manager: George Bamberger
Batting leader: Mookie Wilson, .279
Home run leader: Dave Kingman, 37
Leading winner: Craig Swan, 11–7
All-star: John Stearns

1983   68–94 6th place, 22 games behind Philadelphia (East)
Manager: George Bamberger, Frank Howard
Batting leader: Mookie Wilson, .276
Home run leader: George Foster, 28
Leading winner: Jesse Orosco, 13–7
All-star: Jesse Orosco

1984   90–72 2d place, 6.5 games behind Chicago (East)
Manager: Davey Johnson
Batting leader: Keith Hernandez, .311
Home run leader: Darryl Strawberry, 26
Leading winner, Dwight Gooden, 17–9
All-stars: Darryl Strawberry (starting outfielder), Dwight Gooden, Keith Hernandez, Jesse Orosco

1985   98–94 2d place, 3 games behind St. Louis (East)
Manager: Davey Johnson
Batting leader: Keith Hernandez, .309
Home run leader: Gary Carter, 32
Leading winner: Dwight Gooden, 24–4
All-stars: Darryl Strawberry (starting outfielder), Gary Carter (injured, did not play) Ron Darling, Dwight Gooden

1986   108–54 1st place, 21.5 games ahead of Philadelphia (East)
Defeated Houston, 4–2 in NLCS
Defeated Boston, 4–3 in World Series
Manager: Davey Johnson
Batting leader: Keith Hernandez, .310
Home run leader: Darryl Strawberry, 27
Leading winner: Bob Ojeda, 18–5
All-stars: Dwight Gooden (starting pitcher), Gary Carter (starting catcher), Keith Hernandez (starting first baseman), Darryl Strawberry (starting outfielder), Sid Fernandez

1987   92–70 2d place, 4 games behind St. Louis (East)
Manager: Davey Johnson
Batting leader: Keith Hernandez, .290
Home run leader: Darryl Strawberry, 39
Leading winner: Dwight Gooden, 15–7
All-stars: Davey Johnson (manager), Gary Carter, Darryl Strawberry, Keith Hernandez, Sid Fernandez

1988   100–60 1st place, 15 games ahead of Pittsburgh (East)
Lost to Los Angeles, 4–3 in NLCS
Manager: Davey Johnson
Batting leader: Kevin McReynolds, .288
Home run leader: Darryl Strawberry, 39
Leading winner: David Cone, 20–3
All-stars: Dwight Gooden (starting pitcher), Gary Carter (starting catcher), Darryl Strawberry (starting outfielder), David Cone

1989   87–75 2d place, 6 games behind Chicago (East)
Manager: Davey Johnson
Batting leader: Howard Johnson, .287
Home run leader: Howard Johnson, 36
Leading winner: Sid Fernandez, 14–5; David Cone, 14–8; Ron
    Darling, 14–14
All-stars: Howard Johnson (starting third baseman), Darryl
    Strawberry (starting outfielder—injured and did not play)

1990   91–71 2d place, 4 games behind Pittsburgh (East)
Manager: Davey Johnson, Bud Harrelson
Batting leader: Dave Magadan, .328
Home run leader: Darryl Strawberry, 37
Leading winner: Frank Viola, 20–12
All-stars: John Franco, Darryl Strawberry, Frank Viola

1991   77–84 5th place, 20.5 games behind Pittsburgh (East)
Manager: Bud Harrelson, Mike Cubbage
Batting leader: Gregg Jefferies, .272
Home run leader: Howard Johnson, 38
Leading winner: David Cone, 14–14
All-stars: Howard Johnson, Frank Viola

1992   72–90 5th place, 24 games behind Pittsburgh (East)
Manager: Jeff Torborg
Batting leader: Eddie Murray, .261
Home run leader: Bobby Bonilla, 19
Leading winner: Sid Fernandez, 14–11
All-star: David Cone

1993   59–103 7th place, 38 games behind Philadelphia (East)
Manager: Jeff Torborg, Dallas Green
Batting leader: Eddie Murray, .285
Home run leader: Bobby Bonilla, 34
Leading winner: Dwight Gooden, 12–15
All-star: Bobby Bonilla

1994   55–58 3rd place, 18.5 games behind Montreal (East)
Manager: Dallas Green
Batting leader: Jeff Kent, .292
Home run leader: Bobby Bonilla, 20

AMAZING METS TRIVIA

Leading winner: Bret Saberhagen, 14–4
All-star: Bret Saberhagen

1995 69–75 2d place tie with Philadelphia, 21 games behind Atlanta (East)
Manager: Dallas Green
Batting leader: Rico Brogna, .289
Home run leader: Rico Brogna, 22
Leading winner: Bobby Jones, 10–10
All-star: Bobby Bonilla

1996 71–91 4th place, 25 games behind Atlanta (East)
Manager: Dallas Green, Bobby Valentine
Batting leader: Lance Johnson, .333
Home run leader: Todd Hundley, 41
Leading winner: Mark Clark, 14–11
All-stars: Lance Johnson (starting outfielder), Todd Hundley

1997 88–74 3rd place, 13 games behind Atlanta (East)
Manager: Bobby Valentine
Batting leader: Edgardo Alfonzo, .315
Home run leader: Todd Hundley, 30
Leading winner: Bobby Jones, 15–9
All-stars: Todd Hundley, Bobby Jones

1998 88–74 2d place, 18 games behind Atlanta (East)
Manager: Bobby Valentine
Batting leader: John Olerud, .354
Home run leader: Mike Piazza, 23
Leading winner: Al Leiter, 17-6
All-stars: Mike Piazza (starting catcher), Rick Reed

1999 97–66 2d place, 6.5 games behind Atlanta (East)
Wild card winner
Defeated Arizona, 3–1 in NLDS
Lost to Atlanta, 4–2 in NLCS
Manager: Bobby Valentine
Batting leader: Edgardo Alfonzo, .304
Home run leader: Mike Piazza, 40
Leading winner: Orel Hershiser, 13–12, Al Leiter, 13–12
All-stars: Mike Piazza (starting catcher)

2000   94–68 2d place, 1 game behind Atlanta (East)
Wild card winner
Defeated San Francisco, 3–1 in NLDS
Defeated St. Louis, 4–1 in NLCS
Lost to New York (AL), 4–1 in World Series
Manager: Bobby Valentine
Batting leader: Mike Piazza, .324, and Edgardo Alfonzo, .324
Home run leader: Mike Piazza, 38
Leading winner: Al Leiter, 16–8
All-stars: Mike Piazza (starting catcher; injured, did not play),
Edgardo Alfonzo, Al Leiter

2001   82–80 3d place, 6 games behind Atlanta (East)
Manager: Bobby Valentine
Batting leader: Mike Piazza, .300
Home run leader: Mike Piazza, 36
Leading winner: Kevin Appier, 11–10; Al Leiter, 11–11; Steve
Trachsel, 11–13
All-stars: Bobby Valentine (manager), Mike Piazza (starting catcher),
Rick Reed

2002   75–86 5th place, 26.5 games behind Atlanta (East)
Manager: Bobby Valentine
Batting leader: Edgardo Alfonzo, .308
Home run leader: Mike Piazza, 33
Leading winner, Al Leiter, 13–13
All-stars: Mike Piazza (starting catcher)

SOURCES

The *New York Times*

The *New York Daily News*

The *New York Herald Tribune*

New York Newsday

New York Post

The *Philadelphia Inquirer*

The *Chicago Tribune*

The *Los Angeles Times*

The *Sporting News*

USA Today

USA Today Baseball Weekly

The Sporting News Baseball Registers (St. Louis, Mo.: Sporting News, 1987, 2001, 2003)

The Sporting News Official Baseball Guides (St. Louis, Mo.: Sporting News, 1947, 1961, 1963–2003)

The Sporting News Box Score Books (St. Louis, Mo.: Sporting News. National League 1984–1993, American League 1985, 1987, 1990, 1993)

1963 New York Mets Yearbook (final rev. ed.)

New York Mets Media/Information/Press/Radio/TV Guides 1962–2003

New York Mets Post Season Guide 1998, 2000

Total Baseball, 5th ed., ed. John Thorn, Pete Palmer, Michael Gershman, and David Pietrusza (New York: Viking, 1997)

Total Baseball, 6th ed., ed. John Thorn, Pete Palmer, Michael Gershman, David Pietrusza, Matthew Silverman, and Sean Lahman (Raleigh, N.C.: Total Sports, 1999)

Total Baseball, 7th ed., ed. John Thorn, Pete Palmer, Michael Gershman, Matthew Silverman, Sean Lahman, and Greg Spira (Kingston, N.Y.: Total Sports, 2001)

Baseball: The Biographical Encyclopedia, ed. David Pietrusza, Matthew Silverman, and Michael Gershman (Kingston, N.Y.: Total Sports, 2000)

Biographical Dictionary of American Sports—Baseball, Revised and Expanded Edition, ed. David L. Porter (Westport, Conn.: Greenwood, 2000)

Total Mets, 1962–1996: A Chronicle of 35 Amazin' Seasons, ed. John Thorn, Pete Palmer, Michael Gershman, David Pietrusza, and Matthew Silverman (1997)

Total Mets 2000, ed. Gary Gillette, Matthew Silverman, and Stuart Shea (Kingston, N.Y.: Total Sports, 2000)

The Sports Encyclopedia: Baseball, 22d ed., by David S. Neft, Richard M. Cohen, and Michael L. Neft (New York: St. Martin's, 2002)

New York Mets Inside Pitch (Durham, N.C.: Coman, 2003)

Bill James Presents Stats Inc.'s Major League Handbook (Skokie, Ill.: STATS Publishing, 1996, 2000, 2001)

The Book of Baseball Records, 2000 Edition, by Seymour Siwoff (New York: Elias Sports Bureau, 2000)

The New York Mets: The Whole Story, by Leonard Koppett (New York: Macmillan, 1970)

Philadelphia Phillies Media Guide 1998

1990 Chicago Cub Information Guide

1983 Montreal Expos Guide

1983 San Francisco Giant Official Media Guide

2002 New York Yankees Information and Record Guide

Houston Astros 2002 Media Guide

2001 Boston Red Sox Media Guide

Baseball Cards of the Sixties: The Complete Topps Cards 1960–1969, by Frank Slocum (New York: Simon & Schuster, 1994)

SABR Presents the Home Run Encyclopedia, ed. Bob McConnell and David Vincent (1996)

This Date in New York Mets History: A Day-by-Day Listing of Events in the History of the New York National League Baseball Team, by Dennis D'Agostino (New York: Stein & Day, 1982)

The No-Hit Hall of Fame: No Hitters of the 20th Century, by Rich Coberly (Newport Beach, Calif.: Triple Play, 1985)

The New York Mets: Twenty-Five Years of Baseball Magic, by Jack Lang and Peter Simon (New York: Holt, 1987)

A Magic Summer: The '69 Mets, by Stanley Cohen (San Diego, Calif.: Harcourt Brace Jovanovich, 1988)

The Baseball Trade Register, by Joseph L. Reichler (New York: Macmillan, 1984)

The Great All-Time Baseball Record Book, rev. Ken Samelson (New York: Macmillan, 1993)

Rookie, by Dwight Gooden with Richard Woodley (Garden City, N.Y.: Doubleday, 1985)

Sports on New York Radio: A Play-by-Play History, by David J. Halberstam (Lincolnwood, Ill.: Masters, 1999)

Aaron to Zipfel, by Rich Marazzi and Len Fiorito (New York: Avon, 1985)

Baseball Draft: The First 25 Years 1965–1989, comp. and ed. Allan Simpson (Durham, N.C.: American Sports Publishing, 1990)

The NBA's Official Encyclopedia of Pro Basketball, ed. Zander Hollander (New York: New American Library, 1981)

The Negro Leagues Book, ed. Dick Clark and Larry Lester (Cooperstown, N.Y.: Society for American Baseball Research, 1994)

Voices of the Game: The First Full-Scale Overview of Baseball Broadcasting, Curt Smith (South Bend, Ind.: Diamond Communications, 1987)

The Dickson Baseball Dictionary, comp. and ed. Paul Dickson (New York: Facts on File, 1989)

Backstage at the Mets, by Lindsey Nelson with Al Hirshberg (New York: Viking, 1966)

Hello Everybody, I'm Lindsey Nelson, by Lindsey Nelson (New York: Beech Tree Books, 1985)

The Tattersall/McConnell Home Run Log. Courtesy of SABR.

Queens Tribune

Queens Chronicle

Flushing Times

baseball-reference.com

www.baseballindex.org/

www.ultimatemets.com

www.mbtn.net/

Retrosheet. The play-by-play information used here was obtained free of charge from and is copyrighted by Retrosheet. Interested parties may contact Retrosheet as 20 Sunset Road, Newark, Del. 19711.

ABOUT THE AUTHORS

Ross Adell was born on June 28, 1955, in Jackson Heights, New York, in the borough of Queens. A lifelong resident of Queens, Ross has been a member of The Society for American Baseball Research since 1984 and has been attending Met games since 1964. He calls Shea Stadium his "home away from home." (In fact, one season he was at Shea so often that his parents wanted to give him his own locker in the Met dressing room.)

As a teenager, Ross started keeping score of Met games and also began to compile statistics of the team and selected players, a hobby that carried over into adulthood. He has every Met box score since 1974. He is also a Met memorabilia collector and owns a collection of Met yearbooks, scorecards, and media guides.

Some of Ross's favorite Met players include Tug McGraw, Jerry Koosman, Tom Seaver, Mookie Wilson, Gary Carter, John Olerud, and Mike Piazza. Ross resides in Flushing, New York, approximately two miles from Shea Stadium.

Ken Samelson has edited scores of baseball books, including *The Baseball Encyclopedia*. He coauthored (with Scott Flatow) *The Macmillan Baseball Quiz Book* and revised Joe Reichler's *The Great All-Time Baseball Record Book*. He has also served as associate producer for *Mets Extra* on WFAN radio and wrote a monthly quiz for *New York Mets Inside Pitch*. He lives in Larchmont, New York, with his wife, Liz, and two children, Spencer and Lena, both huge Met fans.

AMAZING
METS TRIVIA